Yale Studies in Hermeneutics

PRAISE OF THEORY

Speeches and Essays

HANS-GEORG GADAMER
translated by Chris Dawson

Yale University Press   New Haven and London

Published with assistance from the Louis Stern Memorial Fund.

This book originally was published as *Lob der Theorie:*
Reden und Aufsätze by Hans-Georg Gadamer,
copyright © 1983 by Suhrkamp (Frankfurt am Main).

Set in Caslon type by Tseng Information Systems, Inc.
Printed in the United States of America.

Library of Congress Cataloging-in-Publication Data
Gadamer, Hans-Georg, 1900–
[Lob der Theorie. English]
Praise of theory : speeches and essays / Hans-Georg Gadamer :
translated by Chris Dawson.
p. cm. — (Yale studies in hermeneutics)
Includes bibliographical references and index.
ISBN 0-300-07310-0 (cloth : alk. paper)
1. Philosophy. 2. Theory (Philosophy) 3. Hermeneutics. 4. Reason.
5. Science and the humanities. I. Title. II. Series.
B3248.G343L6313 1998
193—dc21 98-7115
CIP

A catalogue record for this book is
available from the British Library.

The paper in this book meets the guidelines
for permanence and durability of the Committee
on Production Guidelines for Book Longevity of
the Council on Library Resources.

10 9 8 7 6 5 4 3 2 1

Contents

FOREWORD

To put it the way Jaspers did, we wanted to grasp in what way reason was incarnate in existence itself. And it is that search which has determined my entire philosophical work. Right to my very last years that impulse has held through. . . . We were in search of a way to think in which we could see the truth of things, to discover the truth that was there in each thing before us in the world. And this meant that we were utterly distanced from . . . efforts to control things, to make things, to manage things.

Thus Hans-Georg Gadamer recently described his life's project from 1930 to the present. *Praise of Theory* confirms this self-assessment. Here, first translated in its entirety, thanks to the care and commitment of Chris Dawson, the essays and lectures of the late 1970s and early 1980s that Gadamer collected in *Praise of Theory* represent his ongoing effort to understand how reason is incarnate in existence itself and why it is impossible, for that very reason, to rationalize our existence.

The second, critical aspect of Gadamer's project is more accessible because more familiar. In *Praise of Theory* Gadamer sounds a warning against the dominant superstition of our time: the unwarranted belief that the life-world can and should be rationalized, that is, reordered according to a technological model of applied knowledge. "Technical thinking," he fears, "is beginning to expand into a universal view of the world." On that view, it is not just the business world that should be rationalized by "efficiency experts"; all worlds are best run scientifically, by discovering the laws governing them, and then altering these worlds in calculable ways that will ultimately benefit us all. This kind of rationalization appeals not only to bureaucrats who use "expert opinion" to avoid taking responsibility and exercising judgment; it appeals to everyone who believes that the life-world can and should be managed scientifically to the end of bettering it. In this fantasy, social engineers join forces with all those obsessed with emancipatory utopias—indeed with all who believe that homo faber is blessed with infinite possibility. A new Enlightenment is needed, Gadamer argues, to overcome the old Enlightenment superstition that we can make our world anything we would have it.

What has made this superstition credible is the seemingly unbounded power of natural science. Within the physical world, science has worked miracles, and there seemed every reason to believe its successes could be replicated in the human world simply by transferring its method. In *Praise of Theory*, as in *Truth and Method*, Gadamer means by scientific method the formal procedure of inquiry by which "reality gets made into an object" so as "to break down the resistance of 'objects' and to dominate the processes of nature." Objectification enables control, and such dominion constitutes the proof and fruit of understanding. The only questions are whether human dominion has any limits, whether there is anything that precludes objectification, and whether a form of non-objectifying rationality exists that therefore cannot be subsumed under method.

For Gadamer, we know, it is above all the human sciences that show why method cannot be the universal paradigm of rationality, and that in turn explains why his work in conceptualizing these sciences has made him skeptical, as he says, of "efforts to control things, to make things, to manage things." The life-world studied by the human sciences cannot be objectified—and hence it cannot be controlled, made, or managed—because we belong to it. The belonging endemic to the human sciences hardly proves that, not being susceptible of method, these sciences are not rational—indeed not sciences. Quite the contrary, the human sciences represent a kind of "reason incarnate in existence," a kind of knowledge—Gadamer calls it practical knowledge—that comes from participation rather than distanciation. The importance, indeed the daily necessity, of practical knowledge implies that method has no monopoly on truth. It is in fact quite blind to the truths that lie beyond the horizon of the technological worldview, the truths of the human sciences.

What then is "the human" that is the subject matter of the human sciences? Among the several defining characteristics of the human to which Gadamer has given his attention over the years—language, in particular—the one to which he returns in *Praise of Theory* is the beautiful. Perhaps this is not entirely unexpected, given his suspicion of "making." "Is human society possible at all when work produces only the necessities?" Gadamer asks. "It is worth considering to what extent what the Greeks called *to kalon*, the beautiful in the broad sense of a free surplus and superfluity, is that whereby human society satisfies itself as human." Elsewhere he speaks of "a whole domain, beyond animal self-preservation and beyond nature-the-artist's inexhaustible play of forms. The clever, deliberate creations of free human being bring a constant surplus into human life: play, imitation, rite, ceremony, and all those things that, unnecessary as they are stimulating, we call the beautiful. This is obviously a list that could be extended further, and it enumerates the opportunities that follow from the non-specialization of being human."

What is distinctively human is not "making"—production that serves the end of self-preservation—but rather superfluity that serves no ends, not even human needs. Romanticism located the superfluous and purposeless in the aesthetic, using beauty as a countervalue in the Age of Mechanics even as Gadamer uses it in the Age of Technology. But what Gadamer learns from the Greeks, Plato in particular, is that *to kalon* cannot be confined within the limits to which neo-Romanticism up to the present has circumscribed it. It keeps overflowing the bounds of the aesthetic, spreading out to embrace all those things that Diotime calls the whole ocean of the beautiful (*Symposium*, 210d). In *Truth and Method*, Gadamer shows that the beautiful plays a role in ethics; in *Praise of Theory*, he shows that the specially human impulse toward *to kalon* has a decisive, even defining, place in science as well.

We have seen above that Gadamer's critique of technology continues unabated in this book, but one difference from the earlier work is that here natural science is not conceived merely as "proto-technology," as it were. Science, Gadamer suggests, cannot be reduced to its applications and uses. Rather, what defines natural science as science is its theoretical character. Is it not the case that "science sometimes involves asking basic questions from whose answers no results can be expected that would directly fulfill any purpose? . . . In truth, all research is basic research, and only through a secondary transformation can it address the problem of applying its findings." Scientific theory, then, is a signal example of "all the ways we resist looking only for the useful." If technology is not the raison d'être of science, however, what is? Gadamer answers: "Science exists and is important for no other reason than because it is 'beautiful.' . . . Thus broadly conceived the beautiful (*kalon* in Greek) pertains to all theoretical science. It is the joy of theory, the joy of discovering the truth, that science lays claim to."

In this book, then, Gadamer praises theory as a way of taking pleasure in truth for its own sake but also and equally as a special case of *to kalon*. Such a conception of truth and beauty strikes strangely on modern ears. We are schooled by the arts and the sciences alike to accept the dichotomy between the two cultures, with beauty consigned to the one and truth to the other. Yet, however dissonant, their reunion is absolutely central to *Praise of Theory* and to Gadamer's philosophical ambition as a whole. In Heidegger's terms, that project is the "hermeneutics of facticity"; in Jaspers's terms, it is "to grasp in what way reason is incarnate in existence itself."

The word incarnate is not employed casually here, as the allusion to Jaspers shows. On the contrary, Gadamer means to draw on all the Christian resonances elaborated in the section on "Language and Verbum" in *Truth and Method*. What distinguishes verbum from logos (reason) is what distinguishes Christian incarnation from the concept of embodiment characteristic of Greek religion. "If the Word became flesh and if it is only in incarnation that spirit is fully realized, then the logos is freed from its spirituality. . . . The uniqueness of the redemptive event introduces the essence of history into Western thought, [and] brings the phenomenon of language out of its immersion in the ideality of meaning." Embodiment maintains the distinction between, say, the real Zeus and his mere appearance in the form of a swan; in the incarnation, however, the apparent is real. The Son does not merely appear as man but becomes man, the Word becomes flesh; and, most important, incarnation does not represent a degeneration or concealment but rather a full realization. As verbum, logos is realized in history, not diminished. For Gadamer, then, the advent symbolizes the way reason is no longer ideal, abstract and transcendent but incarnate in historical existence, without at all losing its character as reason thereby.

Gadamer is not a theologian, however, and when he explicates the notion of incarnate reason, he does so not only in

Christian terms—the word becoming flesh. Rather he turns to Plato—hardly a promising source for anyone whose aim is "to discover the truth that [is] there in each thing before us in the world." Yet in Socrates' discussion of beauty Gadamer discovers precisely what one would not expect to find in the great metaphysician: a point of tangency between this world and the other, the intersection between existence and transcendence that corresponds to incarnate reason. "Beauty [Socrates says] shone bright amidst these visions, and in this world below we apprehend it through the clearest of our senses, clear and resplendent. For sight is the keenest mode of perception vouchsafed us through the body; wisdom, indeed, we cannot see thereby . . . nor yet any other of those beloved objects, save only beauty; for beauty alone has been ordained, to be most manifest to sense and most lovely of all." "Mediating between idea and appearance"—this, says Gadamer, "is the metaphysical crux of Platonism," and its locus of beauty. Unlike other ideas, "the idea of the beautiful is truly present, whole and undivided, in what is beautiful." In "this world below," we can be deceived by what only seems wise, say, or what merely appears to be good: but even in this world of appearances, all beauty is true beauty, because it is in the nature of beauty to appear. That is what makes the beautiful distinct among ideas, according to Socrates. It is *ekphanestaton,* most radiant, most manifest. The beautiful appears of itself. It needs no validation other than itself, no signs that could err or lie, because it offers itself in evidence of its own truth. For Gadamer, beauty represents self-evidence, the most fundamental kind of truth. Beauty exemplifies the indivisibility of the real and the apparent; it represents, in Jaspers's terms, reason incarnate in existence.

Whereas method, as Gadamer defines it, is the formal ideal of abstract rationality, the faculty of incarnate reason is something more like taste. In judging of beauty, taste is always situated in existence. It always participates in local, historically determined norms and yet, even when cognizant of its situatedness, taste does not disavow its judgments of the beautiful but on the contrary, as Immanuel Kant proclaimed, expects them to be universally accepted. In this way, taste represents "an ideal of rationality with determinate content," an alternative to the contentless ideal of method. It is not the only one, of course. Once we move beyond the aesthetic, taste takes its place among other forms of *phronesis* no less grounded in the facticity of *Dasein*—"the convictions, values and habits that we all share with the deepest inner clarity and the most profound communality." Yet, for all this, the good judgments of phronesis do not lose their claim to be rational; they are no less logos for being grounded in ethos. There is no standard of certainty higher than the self-evidence of what "we all share with the deepest inner clarity."

But if taste is best understood as a form of practical or incarnate reason in general, what is the case for beauty, once we proceed outward to the "wide ocean of the beautiful"—that is, to being in general? We saw above that it is in the nature of the beautiful to appear. Its mode of being is self-presentation, and in this respect, Gadamer contends, the beautiful is representative of being in general, for the nature of being is to appear: being presents itself in language, especially the language that Gadamer here calls not verbum but *Sage*, the language of poetry and legend. Such language is not semiotic, insofar as a sign involves a signifier representing a signified different from itself. Here they are indivisible. Like English "saga" and etymologically related to it, German Sage unites in its meaning both what is said and the saying of it. It designates "the word's special claim to autonomy, not to be saying something that would then need to be confirmed or certified [by appeal to its referent], but rather something that is certain precisely in its being said."

It is not by chance that legend, poetry, and other nonsemiotic forms of language share the self-evidence of ethos. If a sign is whatever can be used to lie, Sage by contrast is a mode of self-evident truth, where the very saying constitutes evidence of what is said. Like beauty, Sage symbolizes the intersection of the real and the apparent, where being and seeming are indivisible because here being is presenting itself in language.

Praise of Theory, then, represents an extension of themes elaborated in *Truth and Method*, but also a significant advance on them. Wary of attempts to rationalize existence because they assume that reason must be imported from without, Gadamer instead looks for the reason incarnate in existence itself and finds it not just in the human sciences. He praises theory in natural science for its self-sufficiency, its very lack of ulterior motive, and he praises poetry and legend for what is very similar, their self-referential, self-evident character. In *Praise of Theory* Gadamer celebrates the arts and the sciences—the sciences for being a mode of beauty, the arts for being a mode of truth—and he celebrates both together as self-legitimating modes of existence dependent for their rationality on nothing above, beyond, or outside themselves.

Joel Weinsheimer

Translator's Introduction

In the twentieth century, philosophy has been divided between what has come to be known as the "analytic philosophy" of the anglophone world and "Continental" European philosophy. In some ways the division was a strange one. Both traditions appeal to the same classics from the history of European philosophy, to Plato and Aristotle and to Descartes and Kant. Both involved reactions to, and vigorous rejections of, the great metaphysical romantics (Hegel in particular). The traditions even drew on common sources from the late nineteenth century, when both sides of the English Channel were witnessing neo-Hegelian and neo-Kantian revivals. Discussions of problems introduced by Gottlob Frege and Franz Brentano have remained of decisive importance in analytic philosophy. And yet until the last quarter of the century the division remained almost absolute.

In recent years, there has been a growing movement toward reconciliation, or at least toward serious mutual reading and consideration from both sides. In Britain and the United States, more and more university courses involve the study of twentieth-century European philosophy, and bookshop shelves have filled up with the works of Martin Heidegger, Michel Foucault, Jacques Derrida, and Jürgen Habermas. This new study has not come easily to those trained in the ways of twentieth-century anglophone philosophy, however. Analytic philosophy prides itself on its ability to nit-pick thoroughly. Every argument must be watertight, and should preferably be translated into logical calculus in order to compel the reader to accept the consequences or reject the premises. Theories should start small and build on one another, with philosophers working on small problems in the hope of making progress together, without any large idealistic scheme to work within and without any real hope of arriving at worthwhile solutions. What is certainly out of the question is the kind of sweeping, evocative approach to problems that Gadamer takes in this book.

In frustration at the narrow vision of analytic philosophy, some English-speaking thinkers have, in recent years, begun to look more carefully at the alternatives offered in the European tradition. Those who have read Ludwig Wittgenstein have sometimes found that they can occasionally make sense of Heidegger. Political theorists have looked again at critical theory and at neo-Marxism. Some people have even tried to dig a theory of knowledge out of Foucault's historical archaeologies of power. And in the end many have taken one look at what Derrida writes, thrown up their hands in horror, incomprehension, and disgust, and decided to stick to analysis after all. Yet Gadamer is a great deal more comprehensible than Derrida or Heidegger, holds more clearly philosophical views than Foucault, and in my opinion runs into less serious tangles and paradoxes than Habermas. There are a number of issues on which his position is not vastly different from that of such analytic philosophers as Donald Davidson or Charles Taylor, and, as the basis of his philosophy involves the building of bridges in the "fusion of horizons," there is much interesting comparison work to be done.

For the general reader, meanwhile, to anybody unschooled in analytic philosophy, Gadamer reads like a great rhetorician, which is what he really is. His rehabilitation of rhetoric is the principal original element in his philosophy, and he uses rhetoric as much as he advocates it. That is not to say that he uses what he calls the "oily" rhetoric of the modern mass media, which, it is claimed, can compel us to believe whatever the journalists tend to presuppose or take for granted. Gadamer's rhetoric aims not to tackle contemporary issues in contemporary language but to return to our tradition and the heritage of European thought in order to see how our modern presuppositions are arbitrary and in order to find possible alternatives to them.

Because his style is rhetorical, though, we do not find a wealth of painstaking deductive argument or careful stipulative definition in Gadamer's writing. Instead, he tries to convince his audience by showing them plausible characterizations of how things are and interesting possibilities of how they could be otherwise. Gadamer, as a rhetorician, is a speaker first and a writer only when his speeches are transcribed. He has produced only two books as such, and one of them, *Plato's Dialectical Ethics*, was written as a thesis in order to obtain a university promotion. The other, *Truth and Method*, is a difficult text, mostly because Gadamer was so inexperienced at constructing readable books and failed to make the argument of the whole work clear at each stage. Its style sounds chatty, however, and large parts of it are clearly based on lectures and speeches that Gadamer has given. All of his other work originated as lectures, speeches, monographs, conference papers, or short essays contributing to journal discussions. Gadamer's need to have a specific audience to address comes across very clearly, and his aim, like that of Socrates, is always to convince his current audience by appealing to their own ideas, and never to provide an argument that must force any rational person who accepts its premises to accept its conclusions.

This rhetorical approach allows Gadamer certain freedoms that other philosophers deny themselves without, I think, detracting from the quality of his philosophical thought. He is not restricted to arguing about narrow or over-specific questions but can allow his thinking to fly into speculation about those great and ultimate questions that lead most philosophers to the subject in the first place. Without constructing an unstable theory on uncertain foundations, he is able to show how these large questions are related to one another, and to suggest what possibilities we have, as humans, for answering them.

In making these suggestions he has an advantage over most other contemporary commentators and so avoids merely reinforcing some modern prejudice about them with his rhetoric. He is what he would himself call a thoroughly cultivated man, and he is familiar with a vast range of ideas from the whole of recorded history: this allows him to survey the historical changes in the approaches people have made to various problems and to see how the answers given in each period were related to the circumstances in which they were made.

Our own period is no exception to this, and a historical approach can reveal where writers in the tradition have found insights that contemporary circumstances conceal from us. The history of thought is of great importance for Gadamer, then, as he believes that the only way we can avoid the compulsion to believe the prejudices of modernity is to search history for alternatives to them. The one tenet to which he holds constantly in all of his writings is that we have no external viewpoint from which to assess the truth of what we all believe, and that no axioms are available that are sufficiently certain to allow the deduction from them of any unprejudiced truths. For him, this devalues the logical and deductive approach to philosophy, and it inspires his rhetorical return to the historical philosophical, theological and literary tradition.

If we are looking for specific claims supported by watertight arguments, then, we shall find Gadamer irritating and shallow. But if we are looking for ways of approaching really deep questions about the world and our place in it, or if we are looking for some kind of orientation in modern society and are frustrated by the lack of any external viewpoint from which to examine it, we shall find Gadamer's historical rhetoric thrilling and invigorating. In these transcripts of his speeches, he addresses us personally, and his style is never dry or uninteresting. If he leaves us with more questions than answers, his historical summaries always leave us with the impression that at least he has left us with better and more relevant questions about our situation in modern society than we had before we heard him. We are also given new ways of trying to answer them: not really new ways of course, but ways that may well be new to us. Who, after all, would think of tackling the problems of modernity by listening carefully to what Plato or Augustine said? This is Gadamer's approach and when he takes it we often feel that he has opened a window that we closed a long time ago and let the fresh air back into the problems with which we are struggling.

GADAMER'S LIFE

Many readers will find it helpful to know a little about Gadamer himself. I am not going into depth here, but knowing the outlines of his career can shed some light on the content of his thought. In fact, there is a good deal of interesting work still to be done on Gadamer's biography. His autobiography, *Philosophical Apprenticeships*, bears the inscription "De nobis ipsis silemus" (let us say nothing of ourselves), and Gadamer is remarkably true to this principle in relating his own life story through his intellectual encounters with other thinkers. For example, he mentions his two marriages and his two daughters only in passing: we are never told whom he married or when, or even the names of his daughters. He tells about his life through sketches of the personalities and the thought of the various philosophers whom he has known and who have influenced him. And although he does occasionally use anecdotes as philosophical examples, there are not enough of these to form any clear ideas about individual stages of his life.

Hans-Georg Gadamer was born in Marburg on February 11, 1900, and grew up in Breslau in Silesia, now Wrocław, in Poland. His father was a chemist. He was never required to fight in the First World War, as he was too young and Breslau was a provincial town a long way from the front. He began to study a wide range of languages, literature, and "human sciences" at Breslau University in 1918, and the next year he moved to Marburg, where he was influenced by Richard Hamann's art history and Stefan George's poetry. He turned to philosophy, and submitted a doctoral dissertation on Plato to Nicolai Hartmann and Paul Natorp in 1922.

The next year, shortly after he was married, Gadamer spent a term in Freiburg with Husserl and Heidegger, who made a deep impression on him. He then returned to Marburg, where Heidegger also moved to take up a chair. Gadamer apparently survived the years of economic crisis under the Weimar republic without being pressured to become anything other than a post-doctoral student. During these years, according to his autobiography, he became deeply insecure about his own intellectual ability, and all through the 1920s he led a "cloistered life," reading very widely in classical literature and philosophy. He ventured out only to go to seminars, lectures, and reading groups, of which there were many both early in the morning and late at night. It is perhaps not altogether surprising that his marriage did not last.

In 1928, he submitted his thesis on Plato's dialectical ethics (now published under that title) that allowed him to "habilitate"—to become a junior lecturer. During the rise of National Socialism he was attempting to become a professor, but was repeatedly passed over for jobs because, he says, he continued to maintain friendships with Jews. Finally, in 1938, he was given a chair at Leipzig. He survived the war there by not speaking out against the Nazis beyond a few cryptic remarks hidden deep in treatises on Plato. He maintained his friendship with Heidegger, who had left Marburg in 1928 and had been an ardent supporter of Hitler in the early years of his rise, despite the fact that Heidegger (although probably deeply disillusioned with the way events turned out) never expressly recanted his Nazism.

After the war, when first the Americans and then the Russians came to Leipzig, Gadamer was made rector of the university, as he was one of the few professors who had had no connections with the Nazis. He did this job for five years, but the attempt to rebuild a free academic life under communism was no easier than academic life under fascism had been. Finally, just as he was about to leave to take a post in Frankfurt in 1947, he was arrested by the Russians and interrogated for three days. Eventually, however, they admitted to having made a mistake (or rather, blamed it on the German police) and let him go.

In Frankfurt he began to write again, but produced only literary history and analyses of Goethe. It was not until he moved to Heidelberg two years later that he returned to philosophy. Throughout the 1950s he worked on his magnum opus, which brought together material he had been using in lectures for years. *Truth and Method* was completed in 1959 and published in 1960. It drew Gadamer into a number of more active philosophical debates, and in the succeeding years he wrote shorter pieces in its defense, clarifying his position with respect to the attacks made by Jürgen Habermas and Emilio Betti. He also continued to work on Plato, and founded a Hegel Society, his contributions to which led to his book on *Hegel's Dialectic*.

In the 1970s he began to travel every year to America to teach one semester at Boston College, and his writings started to include a greater emphasis on practical philosophy. Most of the essays in this book are the products of this period of Gadamer's career, a time in which his new contact with the English-speaking philosophical community was giving a renewed impetus to his thinking. All of the pieces here were, however, prepared for and delivered to German audiences rather than American ones.

At the time of writing this introduction, Gadamer is 95 years old and is still remarkably active. Although he officially retired from his chair in the 1970s, he still has rooms in the *Philosophisches Seminar* at the University of Heidelberg, where he still gives enthralling public lectures to packed lecture halls without notes, and still attends conferences diligently, offering clear, incisive and amiable commentary on the papers presented. The ten projected volumes of his collected writings are now all available, but Gadamer is still producing new work every time he gives a lecture.

GADAMER'S THOUGHT

It may come as a surprise to those who are acquainted with *Truth and Method* that Gadamer could be the author of a book entitled *Praise of Theory*. After all, he has become renowned for his polemic against the dominance of the methodology of the natural sciences, and "theory" is a word that is immediately associated with that methodology. *Truth and Method* argues that the following of "scientific method," which we might suppose to involve the setting up and testing of theories about the world, is not a privileged route to truth, and that truth itself is more an event that arises within certain kinds of conversation than a property of propositions or theories about the world. Does *Praise of Theory* represent a change of heart on Gadamer's part?

The title itself is, of course, ambiguous. The essay from which the book's title is drawn traces the history of *protreptic,* a name for discourse that exhorts, teaches, and advocates

"theory" in the form of an "examined life." But it is also itself
—as are many of the other essays in this book—protreptical
in nature: it is "in praise of theory" as much as it examines
"the praise of theory." The title already suggests, then, that
Gadamer's aim is both descriptive and normative. He wants to
describe what "theory" and "science" mean to him, and also to
recommend them to us as ideals.

This seems to be a departure from his earlier work in two
ways. Gadamer is now urging us toward science as an ideal,
whereas before he seemed extremely wary of science in general, seeking to demonstrate the primary roles played by art
and history. It is also interesting to find him with such a positive recommendation at all. The aim of *Truth and Method* is
professedly descriptive: the universal and ontological nature of
hermeneutics is brought out in an analysis of play, prejudice,
and understanding, but no normative consequences are drawn.
Reason in the Age of Science raises questions about how we should
respond to the advance of technology, but it is far from recommending that we turn to science. *Praise of Theory* now leads us
to re-examine the concepts of theory and science, and to see
how a genuine scientific questioning can be maintained within
our modern technological culture.

In fact, this has been a concern of Gadamer's for a very
long time.[1] His understanding of the concept of science, like
so much of his philosophical insight, arises from his extensive
classical scholarship, and especially from his reading of Plato.
His earliest concerns were with ancient philosophy, and his love
of ancient Greece remains the driving force behind this book.
Gadamer isolates the Greeks as the only people in the world
to have developed a concern with abstract questioning about
nature and our place in it, and to have separated this concern
from religion and from literature, thus founding both philosophy and science. His interest is therefore always to see how

our modern concepts started out, what they meant when the Greeks first questioned them, and how they remain related to the mythology from which they became separated.

The "theory" that Gadamer praises, then, is not what modern scientists understand by the word. Gadamer has not changed his mind about the shallowness of scientific method in comparison with dialogue and the openness arising from a recognition of our finitude. On the contrary, he counts the Greek notion of theoria alongside art and dialogue as a source of truth because he traces its original meaning as one starkly different to that implied in the slavish following of a method to achieve a result. The encounter with a true work of art is supposed to bring us face to face with our selves and so to lift us momentarily out of our everyday concerns and allow us to experience an event of truth (this is discussed in *The Relevance of the Beautiful*). There is also a certain kind of dialogue, as Gadamer explains in *Truth and Method,* in which the partners in the conversation are aware of their own finitude, aware of the effect that history has on them and on their conversation, and are therefore able to approach the subject matter they are discussing playfully, to bring their prejudices into play by putting them at risk: this allows them to "stand outside themselves" and to be truly present to the subject matter they are discussing. In this way, the movement of their conversation moves them toward what Gadamer calls a "fusion of horizons," and an event of truth. "Theoria" is the element that is common to these two events. It is "being-outside-oneself" so as to be truly present to something else.

How is this notion related to what we call theory? Clearly, it has nothing to do with the notion of a theory, a system of propositions to be tested by experiment and so confirmed or overturned. It is much more closely linked to our familiar contrast between theory and practice; yet Gadamer claims that the contrast is misleading and that theory is, in fact, itself the highest form of practice, the "highest manner of being human" (*Truth and Method*, 454). In tracing back the ancient Greek etymology, he reaches a point where theoria means just "witnessing." Here the idea is intrinsically linked with festive ritual. An important participant in such rituals would be a witness, someone who was there just to see what happened and through this act of witnessing gave the ritual its validity. It was through this theoria, or witnessing, that a festive ritual could be what Gadamer thinks of as an "event of truth." Hence the very act of witnessing was productive, and therefore practical. As we can see from Gadamer's analysis of festivals in *The Relevance of the Beautiful*, the communal element of ritual whereby each individual is caught up by the wider context of events of which she forms a part gives to the act of witnessing its element of "standing-outside-oneself." Theoria involves validating something by being caught up in it, bearing witness to it.

Gadamer traces the continuity of this notion with Plato's idea of the philosophical life. The link is drawn from his reading of Plato's theory of forms, and his reflections on the relationship between Plato's idea of the Good and his mysterious doctrine of ideal number. A closer look at Gadamer's understanding of Plato will help us to see how he views scientific theory.

Gadamer believes that to read Plato as though all of the forms were supposed to be transcendent is a mistake. When Plato says that we need to "look away" from the things around us in order to see reality, Gadamer thinks that all he is really recommending here is a quest for elegant unity among the confused variety of phenomena we encounter. By and large, he says, Plato's forms are simply the same kind of *universalia in rebus* about which Aristotle was to speak.[2] But some of the forms are more transcendent exceptions to this: here Gadamer draws on his interpretation (which is based on the extant dialogues) of the indirect tradition of Plato's thought about number.[3] He takes Plato to have placed great emphasis on the fact that any unity always presupposes a plurality, and vice versa. Thus whenever we have one thing it can be both divided and combined, and either of these processes will give a plurality. Similarly, any plurality, taken together, can be regarded as a unity. Gadamer thinks that Plato understood certain of the forms—those most closely related to the idea of the Good—as having a structure analogous to this. One of these forms is the beautiful, which Gadamer therefore thinks can be wholly present as a unity in each of its many instances: any beautiful thing has a radiant elegance about it, which, although it needs no further justification and arises wholly from the very particularity of the particular beautiful thing, points beyond itself and drives us to look for further elegant unities in other things. In this way, our experience of the beautiful is supposed to turn us toward the Good. For Gadamer, Plato's idea of the Good is identified with unity as such. Thus the purpose of protreptic becomes a display of elegance that turns us to search for unity. Gadamer identifies theoria with the witnessing of unity's manifestation in what is beautiful and good.[4] This witnessing leads us away from the confusion of our manifold sense-impressions, and toward dialectical reflection which aims toward establishing unity.

This reading of Plato, then, allows us to see how Gadamer's notion of theory can be related to modern science. Theoria is both a practical witnessing of something that presents itself as self-evident—a witnessing which is all that is needed to confirm it as true—and also the first step toward a withdrawal out of the confusion of our everyday lives into a contemplation that pursues unity. Gadamer derives his positive idea of science from this basis. A true scientist is someone who pursues the truth, that is, someone who looks for elegant unity that underlies the confusion of our observations: it is also someone who withdraws from the multiplicity of common-sense opinions. This now looks a great deal more like our familiar conception of a theorist. But Gadamer is critical of the idea that it might ever be possible to reach the goal of unity for which a theorist aims: he does not believe that there is any unique truth toward which theories can approach as they are improved. This is consistent with his reading of Plato's idea of the Good as the only truly transcendent form: it is right for us to aim toward unity, but it is always necessarily beyond our grasp, because all unity is always also multiplicity.

In *Truth and Method*, Gadamer shows how his hermeneutic notion of truth is related to art, history, and language. He begins with art because he believes that it is our encounter with the beautiful that first leads us toward the renunciation that is involved in genuine theory. Art is analyzed as free play that is transformed into a structure through its being understood as a unity. This does not mean that an artwork really is a unity: quite the reverse. Only in being understood as a unity by an audience or individual on a specific occasion can art be truly effective, because it is only in these particular attempts at unification that a work of art can have a personal meaning and be applied to the lives of those who understand it. There is no transcendent "true meaning" or "author's intention" behind an artwork, because it is only really effective as an artwork from the points of view of those who find it has a particular meaning for them that is applicable to their own lives. Similarly there are no "true facts" about what has happened in the past. Instead, history is seen as the dimension within which we live: Gadamer emphasizes that we are finite knowers and that therefore no infinite or wholly objective perspective is ever available to us. He avoids advocating a thoroughgoing relativism or "historicism," however, by emphasizing the role played by tradition. Tradition not only transmits accepted historical truths to us but also determines our whole outlook on life by means of the evolution of language. Gadamer sees language not as a conventional structure of signifiers that convey clearly defined meanings, but as a means of direct personal communication that continually changes and evolves as a result of what people try to use it to do. Hence he thinks that our concepts hold within them deep truths about reality, and embody the entire evolution of our tradition. Consequently, conceptual analysis is his favorite means of setting out on his quest for unattainable unity, and he is always trying to look closely at the connotations that our language carries within it.

Again and again in this book, then, we shall find that Gadamer comes to consider some concept, such as tolerance, culture, or reason, in terms of the history of words and concepts. This is an important part of his hermeneutic appropriation of tradition. "Hermeneutics" means just "interpretation," but it has come to be a name for the lines of thought explored by Gadamer, Paul Ricoeur, and other followers of Heidegger. What it points to is Gadamer's emphasis on finite understanding. He consistently refuses to allow any claims to be able to find a universally valid viewpoint, or to be approaching (as opposed to just aiming toward) a description that could claim to be complete or uniquely true. He claims that this analysis is itself universal, however, on the basis that hermeneutics itself is a universal problem that we encounter every time we try to understand one another. Gadamer believes not only that all understanding is tied to the model of one individual trying to understand another in conversation but also that all being that can ever be understood is tied to this situation; thus, the only understanding that it is possible for us to attain is that which we derive by the same essentially linguistic means that we employ there. Because of his refusal to allow any external viewpoint, then, he continually emphasizes the role played by an individual's finite understanding. Even taken together, we remain tied to our finite viewpoints, and so the only truth we can attain is hermeneutic in nature.

But this need not mean that it is impossible for us to break away from the tradition that determines us, or gain sufficient distance from it to criticize the culture within which we live. *Praise of Theory* is full of cultural critique, and we must ask on what basis Gadamer believes that such critique is possible. After all, Habermas and others have argued that on Gadamer's account there can be no critique of tradition, because that tradition is supposed to be the only possible source of our beliefs and prejudices. Gadamer holds that we can never correct all of our prejudices, because the limited nature of our understanding prevents us from bringing all of them into play at once. Habermas and others have argued that this view must inevitably lead to a more or less defeatist acquiescence in the social status quo. The only other possibility, however, is to introduce some sort of theoretical framework or transcendental ideal that can act as an external yardstick against which to judge our current beliefs. Gadamer's worry is that there is no way for us to do this, and that any "external" measure we attempt to construct (such as an "ideal speech situation") must inevitably remain influenced by the very prejudices it is designed to measure.

In *Praise of Theory* Gadamer further emphasizes his idea that what really distinguishes man from animals is our ability to "take up distance" from our immediate situation. In *Truth and Method* and elsewhere, this ability is usually identified with language, which enables us to introduce to one another elements that are not present to our senses, and to discuss them as though they were in front of us. In *Praise of Theory* it is also identified with the theoretical attitude: a theorist can take up distance from her immediate concerns by becoming involved in a quest to learn about something she finds interesting. Theory is thought of as becoming absorbed in witnessing something that has no immediate practical relevance to one's life and situation.

It is an extension of just this idea of distance that Gadamer makes to enable the possibility of cultural critique. What seems to prevent us from being able to criticize the tradition, to which Gadamer has said that we "belong" because it determines our beliefs and attitudes so completely, is our inability to reassess the prejudices it has given us from any viewpoint that is external to those prejudices. But even if we cannot bring all of our prejudices into play at once and reassess the whole package, we can achieve a sufficient level of open-mindedness to be able to re-evaluate a few prejudices at a time. We do this through theory. In *Truth and Method* this process was most often described as becoming involved in a "real conversation" in which the personal concerns of the interlocutors become irrelevant, and they are joined in questioning together about the truth of the subject matter they are discussing. Gadamer also said that it is possible to have this kind of conversation with a text, and that conversation is more productive if the initial prejudices of the two interlocutors are very different. For this reason, he recommends a return to the older texts of tradition in order to enter into conversation with them and to see where our prejudices differ from theirs, in the hope that we may find some new insight. He follows this procedure regularly in this book by consulting classical authors about our modern situation, and quoting them as witnesses to the possibility of a different viewpoint.

But we can see that what is important in this procedure is that it enables us to take up distance from our personal and practical concerns, and that this at once moves us one step away from the full force of our prejudices: if we become involved in theory, in disinterested questioning, it is easier for us to be open-minded and so easier to find new ways of looking at our own situation. If we merely pursue our interests, we shall remain with the prejudices they have given us, but if we turn away from our interests and become involved in "irrelevant" questioning, our whole outlook can easily be changed, and this can have positive results with respect to our actual concerns. Hence we find Gadamer saying that he is not impressed by a researcher who fulfills his research program and succeeds in proving what he wanted to prove: he is much more impressed by somebody who leaves his research plan behind altogether and follows up a side-track that puzzles him and, as a result, finds something altogether unexpected and new.

Hence it is correct to say that Gadamer's position does not allow for the possibility of systematic cultural critique: and this is precisely the reason why we find no systematic criticism either in this book or elsewhere. But he is still able to give us valuable and chastening insights into the way we live and think by holding up the way people have thought in the past as a distorting mirror in which we can view ourselves, which will allow us to see how the mirrors we are used to also present us with distortions.

"Praise of Theory"

The essays that appear in this book were written for various purposes and occasions: as a result, the book contains a certain amount of repetition. But as Gadamer always speaks from memory, and develops his topic anew in addressing each new audience, every time he comes back to a theme we find a slightly new slant on it. This makes every new essay interesting in its own right, even where it covers ground that Gadamer has already dealt with elsewhere. In *Praise of Theory* we find a collection of essays that go well together and read remarkably smoothly, and the repeated recurrence of certain themes such as the Enlightenment treatment of rationality serves to clarify Gadamer's position on these issues to a greater extent than is achieved by any individual essay.

Although most of the essays here are easily accessible and display Gadamer's assured and lucid rhetorical style, in the first essay, "Culture and the Word," we find Gadamer at his most obscure and, at times, his most verbose. The essay is important for those who are interested in the details of Gadamer's position, however, because it deals with themes that are not treated elsewhere. It is in this essay that he endeavors to explain how he sees language as being the unique distinguishing feature of humankind, and in which he explains how he sees philosophy as a product of our specific Western tradition that is derived from classical antiquity. Here he also tries to explain how meaning, even in individual cases, is dependent not on the semantic conventions attached to individual words and constructions, but somehow on the whole of language and the entirety of our ability to communicate with one another. The obscurity of the passages in which he attempts to defend this position is evidence of the difficulty these questions present. His ideas are certainly interesting, but his success, in my opinion, is limited.

It is in the title essay of this collection that Gadamer explains in detail how he takes theoretical and practical concerns to be mutually interdependent. In doing so, he treats us to a sweeping summary of the history of philosophy; here he examines how the tension between involvement in practical and political affairs and the desire to back away from life in order to consider it theoretically has expressed itself in each era of Western culture. He concludes that any practical activity that involves no theoretical reflection on the nature and goals of life is stifling and useless, but that the proper meaning of "theory" is a practical one of being caught up in a communal sharing in "what is," and that it is this that inspires worthwhile practical activity.

This conclusion forms the backdrop for the social commentary he makes in the essays that follow.

In "The Power of Reason," one of the oldest pieces in the book, Gadamer defines reason as the attempt to "identify with the universal." He suggests that to be rational is to go beyond one's own immediate opinions, beliefs, desires, and prejudices and to try to make sense of what other people say. Only in this way, he argues, can it be possible for people to overcome their natural animosity toward one another and to develop the art of compromise: there needs to be some communal element, some force of solidarity to pull us together. The importance of diversity and open-mindedness is a theme throughout Gadamer's writings, and this impassioned attack on dogmatism is as clear and brief a statement of his beliefs on the subject as he has offered.

The theme of rationality is further developed in "The Ideal of Practical Philosophy," where Gadamer argues that the basis of our rationality is a communal practical involvement with one another and the world, and that our common commitment to this must necessarily underlie any attempt to theorize about it. He claims that for this reason, the humanities should not try to emulate the scientific rationality of mathematics and natural science, but should instead try to testify to and share in this background of shared practical rationality, relying on rhetoric as much as on deductive reasoning. Here we also find the further suggestion (as so often with Gadamer, frustratingly left as no more than a suggestion) that the rationality of the natural sciences themselves might ultimately be dependent on their "hermeneutic" background in living practice. He takes up this theme again in his essay on the expressive force of language.

Then, in "Science and the Public Sphere," Gadamer begins to apply these ideas about rationality, theory, and practice to contemporary social issues. He argues that the desire to theorize and to research is as fundamental a part of being human as our practical social and political activity is, and that there is an inevitable conflict between the two. This gives rise to the problem of finding a balance and a compromise between two sides of our nature, which is expressed in the problem of the social role of academia and the funding of abstract research.

In "Science as an Instrument of Enlightenment," we find Gadamer's first decisive criticisms of modern society, and his first recommendations about how matters might be improved. As in *Truth and Method,* his complaint is that the model of scientific method has become too dominant, allowing us to become slaves to a technology that aims only to dominate nature without thinking through what it is doing and why. He calls for us to go through a third Enlightenment in which we lose the prejudices not of myth or of religion but of the "technological dream" and the "emancipatory utopia" (this latter phrase refers to Habermas and critical theory in general). This leads him to deal with the contemporary problems of environmental ethics, and he ends with a plea that we must alter our consciousness so as to think of ourselves as "stewards of the earth."

The centerpiece of the book is Gadamer's historical examination of the concept of tolerance. Here the central ethical themes of the book are introduced as Gadamer discusses the processes of "rationalization" that take place in modern capitalist society. He argues that the eighteenth-century state, which was secure in the authority of the king and the religious morality of the people (so that it could afford to be tolerant of differing religious beliefs), has been replaced by a faceless "system" in which we are all forced to adapt to fulfilling a function that has no meaning for us. He claims that this rationalized system has forced us to lose all the solidarities that once held us together and gave us ethical direction. There are no ethical certainties any more but only a disorientating relativism, and from this Gadamer concludes that one universal ethical requirement must emerge after all—the requirement of tolerance.

In the following essay, Gadamer takes a more analytic approach, and comes as close as he ever does to defining some of his central ethical terms—"Isolation as a Symptom of Self-Alienation." Here we find explanations of what Gadamer means by such phrases as "rational obligation," "administration," and "freedom." This is also where he explains in most detail exactly how communality and solidarity are to be established within modern capitalist society, and how they can help us to break out of the isolation into which it has cast us and to re-establish our connection with "the universal." His answer contains a surprising echo of Marxism, following as it does Hegel's analysis of the relationship between the consciousness of the master and that of the slave. Gadamer's contention is that we can find solidarity only by finding our own self-fulfillment in our work: what he does not make clear, however, is exactly how it is possible to achieve this within the specialized functions into which he has claimed modern society divides us.

In his essay on the significance of the human hand, Gadamer draws some of these ideas together, examining again the possibility of finding an equilibrium between two conflicting sides of human nature. He argues that it is the fact that our senses and our intellect are not naturally specialized that distinguishes us from the animals, and that we must not allow our scientific culture to drive us into an unwanted artificial specialization in our social functions. This artificial specialization, he contends, weakens our power of individual judgment by forcing us to fit in with a pattern that is meaningless to us. His suggested solution to this problem comes in his explanation of his notion of *Bildung* (cultivation) as the developing of a possibility of judging for oneself by coming to be able to see alternative points of view. At the end of the essay, we find the clearest implication Gadamer gives that he believes it to be possible for some individuals to acquire the right kind of cultivation even if our society tends to prevent it, and that they can lead the way toward establishing a communal power of judgment (or *sensus communis*) that can succeed in making the political consultation of the people a more meaningful process, and in allowing governments to acquire a genuine sense of political judgment.

"The Expressive Force of Language" deals further with this sensus communis, relating it back to Gadamer's principal concern in *Truth and Method*—the relationship between language and understanding. In this essay Gadamer defends his use of rhetorical rather than logical arguments on the grounds that it is in rhetoric, not logic, that community and solidarity are forged, and that all logical and scientific reason must rely on a rhetorical background in everyday life, at least if it is to have any social consequences. He discusses how over the past three centuries we have moved away from the ideal of the cultivated scholar who has a very broad knowledge of academic issues, an openness to further inquiry, and the ability to express himself to laypeople in clear and elegant terms. This ideal, Gadamer argues, has been replaced by that of the scientist who is a specialist in a narrow field. This restriction is said to hinder his attempts to express himself to outsiders and consequently to narrow his own vision and weaken his power of judgment: this in turn makes the frequent appeals made to his expertise by the media and the judiciary less and less appropriate.

This contrast between literary and scientific styles of writing is developed further in the concluding essay. Whereas some of the comments in "Good German" are certainly specific to German, there are a good many that are equally applicable to any language. It is a charming essay, and it is fun to note how Gadamer's own writing seems to be more carefully styled than usual when he discusses style. It is also an appropriate place to end the discussion of the relation between theory and practice: Gadamer argues that what is theoretically important in style is to have the practical ability to use the rules and conventions of language to one's own advantage in communicating what one wants to say. Once again, the emphasis is on finding balances, here on those between imitating and diverging and between conceptual and poetic thought.

Gadamer reaches few conclusions in this book, and even his recommendations concerning the ways in which contemporary society can be improved often remain unclear. He is continually seeking useful approaches to our social problems, but thinks that if he were ever to believe himself to have found the answers, this would in itself constitute evidence that he had merely given up the search. Hence not one of these essays ends with a specific conclusion. Far more often, they end with a quotation—usually a quotation about the need to go on searching, or about the limitations of our individual powers and the importance of cultivating our communal judgment. As we have seen, this apparent vagueness is what Gadamer's ideas about understanding and social critique would lead us to expect. But the impression we might get from a first reading, that it is the result of shallow or woolly thinking, is certainly wrong. We must not be deceived by Gadamer's chatty style, which (as the concluding quotation suggests) conceals a wealth of subtle thinking and artistry. Gadamer deals with real and serious problems, and goes only as far with them as he is sure he is justified in doing. If we wish to produce any arguments that claim to be more than the suggestions Gadamer offers, we must show how they can hold any valid claim over anyone other than the individuals or groups that happen to agree with the premises and logic they use. Alternatively, we can follow Gadamer in drawing on the tradition that underlies the differences between so many of us, and in using rhetoric to build a communal solidarity in which we can find balances and compromises that will allow us to make better sense of ourselves and the world we share.

I

Culture and the Word

The concept of culture is suspended in a peculiar indeterminacy. If I were a philosophical poet of Plato's stature, it would not be hard for me to compose a dialogue in which Socrates asked each of us what he really means by culture. And right up to the end of that dialogue, every one of us would be stuck for an answer: although we would all know that culture is something that supports us, none of us would be so knowledgeable as to say what culture is. This points to a deep-seated problem, as we know from the almost indisseverable connection between culture and the critique of culture, between pride in culture and pessimism about culture. Thus, the positively second-hand German word *Kultur* occurs for the first time in an interesting way, in the form of an independent concept, as an Enlightenment concept of value: that one could be lifted up above the rawness of the state of nature and progress along this path to become a perfect "policy maker," toward complete humanity— this was the arrogant confidence of modernity at its beginnings.

The Enlightenment's pride in reason has been contested since Rousseau wrote his famous discourse of 1750, which won a prize at the Academy of Dijon. It dealt with the assigned question: What moral advancements does mankind owe to the unfolding of the sciences and the arts? ("Si le rétablissement des sciences et des arts a contribué à épurer les mœurs"). This question stemmed from the spirit of the Enlightenment, and

A lecture given at the opening of the Salzburg Hochschulwochen, 1980.

in answer to it, Rousseau praised the innocence and simple purity of nature.[1] Kant admitted "Rousseau has set me right,"[2] and grounded the principle of morality on the autonomy of moral reason, which is the same for everybody. Herder followed Rousseau's critique of corrupting customs at least so far as to contrast true culture to civilization.[3] That distinction proved decisive for the German-speaking world and beyond for a long time. The apolitical, aesthetic tone in the word, which can be heard in the phrase "art and culture" and in our concept of "cultural life," arose from this separation of the technical ordering of life (civilized and therefore superficial) from profound culture. Schopenhauer's work became its philosophical expression in modernity, in the nineteenth century in particular. According to Schopenhauer, redemption from the dreadfulness of the blind Will that governs the whole of nature and the human world lies in disinterested viewing, and so in art in particular.[4]

With the rise of bourgeois society, that is with the ascent of the bourgeoisie to equality with the court and nobility, an almost religious cult of art arose. This movement provided the cultural furniture of so-called urban cultural life, whose theaters, museums, concert halls, and lecture halls reveal the enthusiasm for culture of the bourgeois centuries. Then, in the twentieth century, a counter-movement occurred that criticized this bourgeois cultural life. I myself belong to the generation that "went into the woods" as members of the youth movement and utterly rejected the cultural life of the towns, especially the opera. These gestures of protest (even the costumes with the iridescent collars) were harmless. But in the affluent society of the second half of the century, these counter-movements began to take on the forms of militant cultural revolution, and were directed just as much against the political order as a whole as they were against the domination of the church. The age of reproduction, as Walter Benjamin called it,[5] dawned when, through the further development of the technology of reproduction, a veritable flood of stimuli and information poured over mankind, which undermined the aura of the primitive and original. This has made us less and less receptive to what is unusual and demanding in culture and in works of art. The industrial age was founded on the cultural heritage of the bourgeois century. How will it control, alter, and transform this heritage? The age of the Enlightenment questioned even the Christian church, which had been our culture for a whole millennium without expressly knowing itself as culture, and in doing so, marked it out as being culture; this shows us what a serious question we are dealing with. It may be thoughts and considerations like this that unite us here.

If, as a philosophical historian, one wants to contribute to this reflection, one is led back to the origins of culture, to the basic, elemental givens, which are words and language. Words and language obviously stand at the beginning of human history and the history of humanity. The oldest record of the human race, as Herder calls it,[6] describes the divine creation and how it began with the word. How does it come to be there all at once? "And God said: let there be light."[7] Did the word bring the light? Was the word the light? Are words light? Does not light really become light where words are encountered, where runes and dumb inscriptions are deciphered for the first time and begin to speak? Or when drawings, accounts, and stories diligently handed down over the centuries illuminate the darkness of the past for us? "Since we are a conversation and can hear from one another"[8]—in these lines of Hölderlin, mankind's conversation with one another and with the divine sound like a single conversation. Because we are a conversation, we are the one story of mankind. In constantly discovering more early cultures and pre-cultures, more of the oldest traces of human life, and in investigating ethnic islands hitherto unreached by the stream of world-historical tradition, we come to know more and more of this story.

The more we become acquainted with the past and present cultures and traditions of peoples who stand outside our Christian tradition, the more we realize that this is a conversation that, however various its languages, always takes place in human, learnable ones. Man "has" the word, as Ferdinand Ebner expresses it,[9] and that is precisely what distinguishes him from all other natural creatures. That man "has" language is a proposition that (in philosophy, that most characteristic creation of the Greeks) arises with "science," and we encounter it for the first time in Aristotle's *Politics*.[10] Aristotle calls man the living creature that has the logos.[11] This takes us straight to the heart of the matter, and brings us quite close to the primal expression of culture, the word.

To be sure, logos does not mean "word," but "discourse," "language," "account;" ultimately, it is everything that is articulated in discourse, thought, and reason. Thus the definition of man that has come down to us through the centuries is that of the *animal rationale,* the creature that has reason, confirming at every stage the latest pride in reason. But logos is not "reason" but "discourse"—precisely words that one person says to another. It is not an accumulation of words like the classified fragments that form the dictionary or so-called *Wörterbuch* (literally, "book of words"). Rather, the logos consists of words already disposed toward the unity of a sense, the sense of discourse. We call that the unity of the sentence. But a sentence too constitutes a fragmentation of the word. If not an entirely artificial one, it is, strictly speaking, an arbitrary unity. For at what point has somebody completely said the words he or she wants to say? Where does the sense end? In the unity of the sentence? Surely, rather, in the unity of the whole discourse that ends in falling silent. Does not the sense of what is said get across completely only when we fall silent, and does it not first begin to expand in the stillness of its having been said? Ultimately, don't the words first come to exist in the answer? Isn't it then that they first become the words that were said to someone and to which someone has had to answer? Or are these words, too, still an abstraction? Is every word in the end an answer? Are we not always answering when we venture a word, by which I mean are we not trying to respond to the other, to the occasion, to the issue, to the *causa*? In any case, the Greek expression "logos" points toward the domain of such a correspondence: it is not for nothing that the aforementioned definition appears in Aristotle's *Politics,* in that great succession of lectures on the basic political constitution and specific character of humankind, where Aristotle subjected human life in its social forms of order and organization to his genius for observation.

The sentence with which this quotation opens already shows the sweeping horizon in which human activity takes place, the horizon of nature:

> [N]ature makes nothing in vain. But out of all living creatures only man has language. The sound of the voice certainly indicates [the oppression of] pain and [the elation of] pleasure and therefore also occurs in other living creatures. That is to say, nature has progressed so far that they have sensations of pain and pleasure and can show it to one another. Language (discourse, logos), on the other hand, is designed for exposing what is helpful and what is harmful, and so also what is right and what is wrong. For what is special about man as against other living creatures is that he alone has a sense of good and bad, right and wrong and such things, and it is communality (solidarity) in these things

that distinguishes [the creature of] the house and the city.[12]

A noteworthy last sentence.[13] Here it is man's having language that sets off his form of life from that of certain kinds of herd animals. His communication is not just the expression of a particular condition—as with, say, birds' warning cries and mating calls—it manages to make manifest what is helpful and what is harmful. That means pointing out things that we want to recommend or warn against even when they do not immediately recommend themselves, perhaps because they are not very pleasant. One thinks of bitter medicine, or of the doctor's painful surgery, which requires a distance from what is present and a looking forwards to what is coming. One is no longer given over and delivered up to the rush of the moment. This, then, is what we recognize in the essence of language: a distance by means of which, in the breath of our voice, fleeting as it is, we can embody everything that occurs to us, making it audible and communicable to others. Obviously, it is this kind of distance with respect to ourselves that opens us up to the other, and enables not merely expressive gestures, or the mere warning cries and mating calls that the animals make to one another, but genuine efforts towards communication. The German word for "communication" is *Mitteilung* which means literally "sharing with." What a beautiful word! It involves the idea that we share something with one another that does not become less as a result, and perhaps even becomes more.

So by way of beginning, culture can be understood as the domain of all that becomes more by sharing it. The external goods of life are the kind of things that isolate us, and where they alone are in view they plunge us into the gloomiest solitude of the ego: Ferdinand Ebner, again, has had profound things to say on this subject.[14]

The word is communication, sharing in its purest form. It is not the voice of pain or pleasure that is extorted by nature, so to speak. It rests on free agreement, *kata syntheken*, as Aristotle has it.[15] But that doesn't mean that it's a real agreement that people settle on in some way. Nor does it mean that the word becomes word through a "significance-bestowing act," as one modern philosopher has termed it. Nothing gets founded here and nothing gets bestowed; we are always already in agreement. It is only through this agreement that the word is word, and is confirmed by every new instance of language use. We are all familiar with the wonderfully touching illusion of parents who celebrate their child's first word, though it's a word that does not exist. There can be no first word, there is only being-able-to-talk, there is only "the" word. The child's first babbling attempts at imitation are not yet a real step toward engaging in the exchange between you and me, surpassing the dumb exchange of glances.[16]

The word first raises communality into words, as it were. The right means to an end is not just what happens to be suitable, but something selected for its suitability, like a tool designed for a particular use. And in this respect the word, as the right means, belongs to the common world; the world of ends itself is correctly defined only as what is suitable and useful to all in common, the *koine sympheron*,[17] as the Greeks said. Revealing what is good in the sense of useful is obviously much the same as revealing the good in the sense of right or wrong. In Aristotle's text, good in the sense of useful is followed by the simple phrase "and so also with right and wrong," as though it were self-evident.[18] To be sure, it is nature that has equipped and organized man in such a way that, unlike animals, he sets up his own equipment and organization in his houses and cities. But what he sets up in this way is not nature, nor is it discourse and words. These things exist by reason of agreement.

Aristotle, the person from whom we are trying to learn here, found a second word that we all use now and that gives expression to this truth. It is not only language that belongs to this domain of common validity and is to that extent nomos (*syntheke*)[19] — the whole of the social life of man is dominated by these validities, which are not necessarily laws, but regularities existing in usage. To describe them, Aristotle found the word from which the word "ethics" is derived: *ethos*. "Ethos" is originally nothing more than a habituation that has become second nature.[20] We talk also of animals' habitual lives. But when we talk of ethos and of the possibilities of ethics, we mean more than merely "established habits." We mean a self-conduct and a bearing that can give an account of itself and answer for itself. It is man's greatest honor and at the same time his greatest peril that he is the one who chooses, so much so that he (so to speak) "undertakes" his whole life.

The Greek expression for this undertaking is *prohairesis*. We "lead" our lives, and so ultimately we try to realize the good — the most proper, most appropriate life — on the basis of our own choice. Nonetheless, it remains the case that human ordering and shaping is always already embedded in the horizon of nature. It is just as little the case that there is a first step toward mankind's achieving culture, as that the babbling child utters a word when it offers the first gifts of affection to its parents. There can be no abstract projection of our whole individual and social life.

In Plato's utopian state we find a portrayal of an idyllic self-sufficient community, where nobody is in conflict and there are no unsatisfied needs.[21] Everyone exists together in wonderful innocence, and their activity is coordinated by easily satisfied regulations. Now Plato, or his Socrates, calls this a city of pigs.[22] The expression "city of pigs" does not quite have our associations of vulgarity and pitiful luxury, but rather just means lack of cultivation, of *paideia* (education). What Plato means to say by calling this idyllic state a city of pigs is that such a state is not at all concerned with the authentic task of man, which consists in ruling and honoring service. The task of man (and of politics) consists in having power and not abusing it just in order to increase it. That is the great lesson of Platonic philosophy: only paideia, only education, can overcome man's deep-rooted instinct of aggression. We are familiar with this as the problem of all politics from Plato to Freud, and it is the hope of all thinkers from Plato to Freud that someday our instinct of aggression might successfully be brought under control, so that Christianity's commandment of love would be taken in earnest.

In the Greek expression paideia, there is an echo of the light-heartedness and innocence of children's play.[23] Its authentic "object," if we can apply this word at all, is the beautiful. But that just refers to everything that commends itself without being of use for anything, so that nobody asks what its purpose is.[24] In its broadest sense, "the beautiful" encompasses nature and art, customs, actions and works, and everything that communicates itself and, in being shared, belongs to everyone.

There is a reason why the word "culture" springs to mind in this connection. Our self-consciousness and its verbal articulation were fashioned by Roman culture. When we say "nature" or "culture," we are speaking Latin. For a rural people like the Romans, "culture" self-evidently referred to agriculture, *agricultura*. Now, when the Roman people learned something new from the Greeks, from Stoic Greek humanity, this word also came to provide the soil in which it grew. Cicero spoke first of the *cultura animi*, cultivating the mind.[25] Even when he did so, the rural way of thinking of this whole linguistic world continued to assert itself in the new concept of cultura. It is as though it is embossed with the stamp of the care and concern of agriculture between sowing and harvest. In the word "culture," and in the essence of culture itself, we are presented not just with the pleasure of free play, but also with the toil of the sowing and harvest of the spirit: cultivation (*Bildung*) toward humanity.

These etymological observations bring us back to a point from which we can see quite clearly what distinguishes the possibilities and dangers of humankind. "Culture" is sufficiently serious that it does not just mean organized free time. What a terrible phrase that is, already indicating that we are not free enough to have free time! Culture is not the organization of our free time: it is all that stops men from assaulting one another, and from being worse than any animal. Worse. For animals, unlike men, know no war: no other species fights with its own kind to the point of annihilation.

So what kind of equipment does man have? And why should we follow the ancient thinker[26] in according such decisive status to "words"? After all, there are also other symbolizations whereby man distinguishes himself from all the animals. He can also recognize himself in the tools, monuments, and emblems that he creates and surrounds himself with. Language is not the only symbolizing activity. Thus Ernst Cassirer once suggested the following as a definition of culture: the universe of symbolization, the symbolic universe.[27] It is true that taking up "distance" belongs as much to the symbolic universe in general as to the word. In "taking up a distance," the word achieves two things for us: recognition of oneself in another, and recognition along with others of what is affirmed by everyone—in our cooperation, in our goals, in our bringing about what is just—even if it is difficult and demanding for each individual to concede or renounce certain things. Wherever man has impressed his design on things, he can certainly be recognized in his tools and structures. It is only in the word, though, that we seem to reach the all-embracing empire of spirit, as it were, which can come into its own in the word, insofar as everything is susceptible of being worded. Thus the word is the highest form in which mankind can shape its world and its fate, the great final syllable of which is called death, and its hope, God.

The mystery of human cultural tradition rests on the word. The expression "tradition" itself is bound tightly to the word, and for good reason. What we immediately understand by "tradition" is the written information that has come to us through writing, copying, and reproduction.[28] Of course, there is also oral tradition, and today we are no longer as convinced as we were about fifty years ago that poetic creations are preeminently written: we have now found out how long a tradition of oral legends survived in the Albanian mountains. Since then, we take seriously the possibility that discourse can become art not only through the medium of writing but also through *mneme*, through *memoria*, through memory. Yet writing, and the resurrection of the words out of writing, remains one of the greatest mysteries of all human tradition. Our very own culture, that of the humanist-Christian tradition, gives us reason to think that this is the case, especially now, when the other great world religions and world cultures are just beginning to engage in a first hesitant conversation with us, and above all now that the massive dialogue that is opening up between atheism and the religions has reached its hour.[29]

So we should once again make ourselves aware of what is specific to the Christian-humanist tradition. Nowhere does this become so clear as in the word. If I were asked to classify the traditions of other cultures, and perhaps had to say whether the great Chinese sage Lao-Tse's[30] words were religious literature, philosophical literature, or poetry, I would not be able to give an answer; not because I do not know, but because it is only in the history of Western civilization and culture that these three forms of discourse and the word have been disentangled and developed, through continuous interchange of ideas with one another.

If I had to name these three kinds of words that have distinguished our tradition, I would say that there is the word of the question, the word of the legend, and the word of the reconciliation and the promise. It is worth examining these three forms of discourse—both independently and in their mutual harmony.

The word of the question[31] is a restless word that reaches from the Greeks' appetite for questioning all the way to the thirst for knowledge of our ever-progressing research. Perhaps the clearest way to characterize this appetite for questions is to say that this word constantly outlives itself. Questioning is what enables us to own up to our finite contingency, and to the limitedness of our knowledge, interpretation and foresight; in short, through it, we own up to the human situation in the world. In modern times, human knowledge and science recognize themselves in the form of the self-outstripping question, in puzzles and questions that continually beget themselves anew; the words "knowledge" and "science" themselves have taken on this connotation of research, of the further questioning that constantly outstrips itself. But the Greeks began with the old, immense questions: "Why is there anything at all rather than nothing?" "What is in the beginning?" "What is chance?" "What is this wonderful pattern of the paths of the stars—and then again, what is this irregularity that we encounter in the night sky, in that all the stars do not complete the prescribed revolution about the center of our earth together but some seem to stray about and are therefore called the planets?"[32]

We think next of our civilization with the new kind of science that arose in the seventeenth century, which no longer wants to integrate itself into the older human knowledge, and keeps inventing new possibilities for forward-looking questioning, abstract constructions, and technical accomplishments and forms of control. Our sciences are the true planets of our human wisdom, and the task for our culture, like the puzzle of the wandering stars for the Greek astronomers, is to tie the planets of the knowledge-cosmos we call "sciences" back into a system, to discover in them the organization that governs what is, and to recognize the ordained place of human beings in the whole of what is. All of this is the word of the question, which continually poses itself in the most varied languages and the most varied traditions, and is always looking for a new answer.

But alongside it stands the other word, the old rival of the Greek religious and philosophical tradition, the poetic word of poetry and legend. Of course "legend" is used in a fairly emphatic sense here, and means more than just the mythical form of information usually called "legend" (*Sage*) in the epic memory of humankind. "Legend" here designates in its entirety the word's special claim to autonomy, not to be saying something that would then need to be confirmed or certified, but rather something that is certain precisely in its being said. That is the age-old meaning of *mythos*, a word that for the most part gets used somewhat inaccurately. Mythos is that which displays its authentic power of truth only by being said repeatedly, and not by being rigorously questioned on the strength of a certainty situated outside the tradition of the legend. Thus a poem is legend, in the sense that the word no longer refers to anything outside (German specialists speak of *Referenz* here). Rather, everything gets gathered into what is said, as it were. Now, this kind of legend is the word at its most authentic—it is word to such an extent that it becomes impossible to separate its significance from its sound. Hence the ideal of poetic legend is fulfilled in its untranslatability. Gathered into the unity of word and sound, the word of the poem is the image of a self-enclosed world, not of a part of the world or of anything in the world. Even something like Eduard Mörike's famous poem on a lamp[33] is not just an early nineteenth-century object-poem or thing-poem that says something about the world, but it is itself world, our world, the world of man that, in what is said, fulfills itself to the point of self-representation in sense and sound. "What's beautiful, though, shines as if blessed in itself"—so goes the last line of this very poem.

Finally, within the limits appropriate to a philosopher, I should say something about the word in the sense of the promise. There are, I think, two human experiences of this word that we all share, even those of us to whom the gift of faith is not granted: the word of forgiveness and the word of reconciliation. We all know something about the factical reality of such a word. We all know what a huge task forgiveness is for the person who forgives. It is really necessary to accept the person who has asked for forgiveness in such a way that he or she is already forgiven. That is the only kind of forgiveness there is: a word that no longer needs to be said because it has already paved the way from the one to the other, because, through the gesture of the word, it has already overcome the discord, the injustice, and consequently everything that divided us.

We turn to the second example of human experience that I mentioned: reconciliation. In the experience of reconciliation, something of the true inner historicality of man presents itself, as does something of his inner possibility of development; so it is one of the deepest experiences that people can ever have. For wherever there has been disunity, discord, and disintegration, wherever we have fallen out with one another, wherever our sociability has collapsed—whether it is between an I and a you, or a person and a society, or perhaps the sinner and the church—we always experience how the reconciliation brings an increase into the world. That is the mystery of reconciliation. Only through reconciliation can the otherness—the insuperable (*unaufhebbare*) otherness that divides man from man—be overcome, nay, raised up (*heraufgehoben*) into the wondrous reality of living and thinking in community and solidarity.[34] Thus it also communicates the Christian message that only through the acceptance (called faith) of the ultimate reconciliation of the crucifixion, can we overcome the ultimate otherness of our mortality, our being doomed to die.

It seems to me that our cultural tradition charges us with the task of nurturing the three forms of the word that I have distinguished, as a pledge of their continuance: the word of the question that outstrips itself, the word of the legend that corroborates itself, and the word of the reconciliation that is like a first and a last word.

2

Praise of Theory

The ancients practiced the festive custom of eulogy, in which recognizably laudable things received public praise: Gods and heroes, love or fatherland, war and peace, justice, wisdom—even old age, which used to be something laudable and not, like today, something almost shameful, a defect, a cause of embarrassment. The lovely custom of eulogy, belonging to a world cognizant of its ideals and sure about them, nurtured a whole genre of eloquence that was considered an undisputed good. It was devoted to praise of such things.

The life inclined to theory was one of the objects of eulogy, and since the days of Socrates and Plato, there has been a genre both of discourse and writing called "protreptic," speeches or writings that celebrate theory. The old name for theory that appears in these titles was admittedly different: philosophy, the love of *sophón*, of true knowledge, of knowledge of the truth. Plato was the first to designate and define a life devoted to philosophy, to pure knowledge, as the "theoretical" ideal of life, and precisely in so doing he challenged the norms of his home city, Athens, and its society. For the Athenian citizens—unlike the working classes of metics[1] and slaves—were understood as being "free" for politics, for active participation in public life. It might also befit a growing boy—girls were never considered—to devote a few years to theory and music: and so these were a mere means of passage and maturation, of education appropriate to the phase of childhood. Even their name—paideia,

A speech given in Bonn, 3 June 1980.

pedagogy—still retains a reference to the child's stage of life, to *pais,* and play (*paidia*).

Entering life meant entering the practice of politics. So the word "theory" already tells us something about the thing it refers to, about the concept itself: its proximity to mere play,[2] to mere looking and wondering at something, far removed from all use, profit, and serious business. In this respect the concept of theory is defined by contrast to the word "practice," and this brings it into the context of the oldest experience of life, one that appears in the common maxim that Kant himself once dealt with: "That might be true in theory, but it doesn't work in practice."[3] The praise of theory becomes a rebuttal of the opposed word "practice." This was already the case in its Greek beginnings. Do we still have occasion to listen to this rebuttal? I confess that on the basis of my own scholarship I am tempted to answer "yes" to this question. What did this praise look like then?

In the early stages of human cultural development and organization of life—whether in Egypt, Babylon, or wherever geometry, algebra, and astronomy were pursued—it is clear that the bare desire for knowledge represented an exception, requiring justification by appeal to religious or practical interests. Also, the first Greek "philosophers," other than Heraclitus, were presumably fully active citizens of their cities, and often their reputations were based largely on their economic or political far-sightedness. Thus Plato's abstinence from politics, with the word "theory" blazoned on his shield, certainly offered a challenge, as did the foundation of the academy. This was life-long school, membership in which seemed to require retreating from politics and embracing the ideal of the theoretical life, and it encouraged "philosophers" to be of no use for practical politics. Socrates' persistent question about the good, and espe-

theory against politics

cially Plato's elaboration of it, tying it to the abstractions of mathematics and dialectics, must of itself have appeared out of place to the practitioners of politics and their sophistic lawyers.

In his ideal state that turns everything on its head, and especially in the famous allegory of the cave, Plato offered a monumental response to their doubts. According to him, the empiricists and pragmatists live in a shadow world projected by a fire behind them that they take for the real world, and they must be freed by force—the force of thought—from their fetters, turned around and compelled to ascend into the light of day and the real sun. There, to be sure, they at first experience prolonged blindness that lasts until they adapt to the brightness and can look at the true world—the world of enduring thoughts. But if they were then compelled—perhaps by civic duty—to turn back into the cave, they would once again be blinded—though in fact only briefly—and would be unable to foresee the consequences of things as well as those accustomed to the darkness of the cave. For this reason those in the cave consider the whole ascent to knowledge to be useless and pernicious: that is how Plato explains why politicians hold theory in such disrepute.[4] To be sure, all this took place on the eve of the free Greek city-state's final downfall; and it was barely still true of the community for which every citizen lived.

But perhaps Plato had something in mind in describing theory-based education that is true for all times. Not only did education come to be occupied with theory ever afterwards: this theoretical schooling was what Europe really inherited from classical antiquity. In the modern state our presupposition of bourgeois civil rights has broadened the concept: both into universal compulsory education, on the one hand, and, with the idea of *Bildung* (cultivation),[5] into a demand for adult education on the other hand. The concept of "Bildung" still retains something of the expectation that a theoretical occupation with

things that "do not concern" one, that are "free" from any calculation of use or utility, should be part of professional training
and belongs with the practical abilities required for it (not least
in administration and civil service). In the paradox of the philosopher king, Plato articulated a lasting truth: being fit to rule
over others or to carry out any official function can mean only
knowing what is better and knowing how to perform the demands of one's office. So the ideal of the theoretical life does
have political significance.

But what Plato has given us is no more than a friendly hint:
we have to continue the struggle over the ideal of a theoretical
life that has been a part of our culture since the Greeks. The
most recent phase of this struggle is now forming itself into a
philosophical concept whereby practice and the thinking that
can prove itself only in serving practice lay claim to a superior
legitimacy. From the point of view of this concept, to praise
theory as such seems completely unacceptable.

Although he celebrated the theoretical ideal of life, Plato remained a citizen of his city. Even if he was a frustrated or failed
politician, for him theory and politics remained indissolubly
united. As the culture of the Greek city-state broke up into the
larger Hellenistic realms and into the Roman Empire, however,
this was to change. Aristotle wanted to legitimize the proper
balance of both, the ideal of the practical and political life and
the priority of the theoretical one, and it would certainly be
wrong to dismiss the priority he accords to theoretical life as
being merely inherited from Plato. Aristotle was probably the
first to show how the practical and political question about the
good is independent of the older, theoretical one that revolved
around cosmology. He opened his investigation of human practice, his Ethics, with the pithy sentence: "Every art and every
inquiry, and similarly every action and choice, is thought to
aim at some good."[6] But he is just as convinced that the theo-

retical interests that inspire every person need no justification. The first sentence of his Metaphysics reads: "By nature all men desire knowledge"[7] — by nature, not just in order to master existence and preserve life but also just to fulfill our own nature, to achieve happiness. The priority of knowledge is recognized even where everything depends entirely on the practical outcome, which is the case whenever knowledge is applied — the classic example that Aristotle had in mind, as a doctor's son, was medicine. The aim of knowledge is fulfilled in mathematics, which deals with unchangeables, but is genuinely fulfilled only in philosophy, which contemplates the permanent essences of things in their very origins — their principles, as we call them.

Man's greatest joy is in "pure theory." This is attested to by the very fact that we are awake, that miracle of our vegetative rhythm that means we can see and think, and so that we are "there." Even the divine can move or fulfill itself in nothing but enjoying the "there" which it is for itself.

Yet Aristotle well knew that it is not only in the joys of knowledge, of insight, of understanding things and people, measures, numbers, the world, and the divine that human self-understanding is fulfilled; he was also concerned with the diversity of human practices, which raises man above the constraints that bind other living creatures, and lets him as a social creature fashion his own ties, customs, and orders. Man stands out in both respects — in the construction of social practice, and in being given to pure knowledge, seeing and thinking. He is the creature who has the logos: he has language, he has distance from the things that immediately press upon him, he is free to choose what is good and to know what is true — and he can even laugh. He is a "theoretical creature" to the core.

In the course of historical life, this fact has been given different emphases. After the first glimmer of the private began to appear in ancient life, a person might withdraw from public life like a Stoic; or he might take his place in it and yet, even as a ruler of the world, hold on to communion with himself as the proper task of his life. Or perhaps with the Epicurean, one might resist the seductions of knowledge and research in order to guard the tranquil peace of the garden, or, moved by the religious longing of the age, he might gradually sink back into positing a divine basis and origin for the world. Whatever the case, it all involves "seeing" (*Schauen*): from the contemplation (*Beschaulichen*) of inner freedom, through the intuition (*Anschauen*) of the great world-order, to the beholding (*Schauen*) of the divine. The Latin equivalent for theoria, contemplation, seems more and more adequate to the whole of this theoretical ideal of life.

Contemplatio—the *vita contemplativa*—came to be defined as opposed to the *vita activa* when the spread of Christianity led to the eclipse of the old gods of the world behind the otherworldly God, so that the world itself no longer shared in the reverence accorded to the gods. The ultimate goal could no longer be to investigate it and get to the bottom of it out of a pure joy of questioning and thirst for knowledge. From then on, the world was thought of as God's divine creation, as the expression of his omnipotence, wisdom, and goodness, and insofar as it is included at all in the contemplatio with which the soul turns toward God, it is nothing but a mirror, a *speculum* of God: contemplatio is at the same time *speculatio*.

This not only turned man's theoretical passion away from the world and back toward God, it at the same time revalued the elemental thirst for knowledge to which Aristotle could still appeal in complete innocence: the craving for knowledge becomes curiosity (*Neugier,* literally "greed for novelty"), *curiositas.*

It is true that the *mirabilia,* the wonderful or the great wonders of the world, were always a source of knowledge about the world and an invitation to explore foreign parts, from the sailors' tales in the *Odyssey* up to Pliny's *Natural History*.[8] But that was never Neugier or curiosity, the mindless gaping that is always drawn in by the newest thing and never dwells on or gets absorbed in anything. Nothing goes out of date so quickly as what is merely new and nothing else. It asks much of human nature to be suspicious of the desire for knowledge as curiosity. A radical devaluation of the visible world stands behind it, as expressed in Augustine's polemic against curiositas.[9]

Again, words tell us a whole story. It goes without saying that what is new is always ambivalent and gets taken up in contrary ways. But it is still significant that this devaluation of the new is rarely encountered among the knowledge-hungry Greeks. Even the Latin equivalent, curiositas, is not used primarily in a negative sense: it is derived from *cura*—care and laudable concern. Even if *curiosus* could also, in this basically rural language, have the devalued sense of "Neugier," and if forward-looking carefulness means being sure to keep a safe distance from the kind of unwelcome novelty that can come in the future, the tone is nevertheless still one of care and providing for the future and precisely not one of greed (*Gier*) for what is new (*neu*). The anti-gnostic position of Ambrose and Augustine was what first gave curiositas its univocally negative meaning.

Now it would certainly be wrong to attribute to the church a general prohibition of theoretical interests. In the end, the preference for the contemplative life, which lay behind the monasteries, was largely what carried on the tradition of Greek culture and knowledge. What would we know about antiquity without the monks' diligent writing? But it is clear that this pious activity consisted more of care for the *litterae* than development of their own research or theoretical energies. God was and remained the proper object of contemplation.

When the new science took the path of methodical rigor, it

ignited a true explosion that burst apart not only the Middle Ages' geocentric view of the world, but also its theocentric one. In the seventeenth century, after Galileo, the mathematical construction of idealized relationships of motion was elevated into the method of knowing reality. It succeeded in constructing classical mechanics, which in the end, thanks to Newton's combining it with celestial mechanics, ushered in a new sense of the world that also changed the ideal of the theoretical life: knowledge became research.

This means something new in two ways: "science" becomes anonymous and vast. "Science" no longer takes on its shape and reality within the individual researcher; he is one of the many whose research contributes to science but at the same time overturns what was previously held "true." "Knowledge" becomes something that is constantly overcoming itself. It is no longer *doctrina*—knowing, teaching, and learning what is true.

But this means, second, that it becomes a great venture, penetrating unknown realms where neither man nor gods can get a foothold. The path it takes—methodical research—involves reason's making sure for itself. For only a malevolent God could lead "science" entirely astray—and then only if he could confuse our mathematical reason. The speculative contemplation of the divine creation in its sensuous fullness, where God's wisdom can be worshiped, is now no longer at issue—mathematical abstraction discovers lawlike relationships hidden from the senses. Only by converting empirical knowledge into mathematical can the researcher approach the goal of understanding the book of nature written by God's hand, a goal that can never be conclusively reached.

By subscribing to the logic of research and so presenting itself as self-certifying, the interest in theoretical knowledge understands itself as extending humankind's power by way of knowledge. It is a matter of course that precisely in the age of science the tension intensifies between abstract and universal theory—which not only emerges with the dignity of science but impels the standardization of practice—and established practices that have become firmly rooted through long habituation. It becomes the struggle of tomorrow's science against yesterday's science, which is supported by the practice of administration. Does practice itself know nothing?

We must ask a double question: Is there perhaps more to theory than what the modern institution of science represents to us? And, is practice, too, perhaps more than the mere application of science? Are theory and practice correctly distinguished at all when they are seen only in opposition to each other? It is true that even in the eighteenth century the Enlightenment's optimism about progress did not go undisputed. Rousseau, Herder, and Kant brought the limits of "pride in reason" to general awareness.[10] When Kant, in the passage quoted at the beginning of this chapter, champions theory against the mistrust of practical men, he does not mean science and its application to practice but the precedence of theory within practice itself: what a human agent knows unconditionally to be his duty and recognizes purely out of reason, as opposed to the faltering and uncertain calculations of self-advantage, is also precisely what is right in practice. In fact, practical reason can restrain rampant pragmatism, just as the *Critique of Pure Reason* refuted the untenable hair-splitting of the rationalist dogmatists. Growing from the Kantian impulse, German idealism tried even more fundamentally to reinstate the concept of "science" in its full richness and to ground the unity of the theoretical and the practical philosophy of science on the primacy of practical reason. Here "science" still has the sense of "knowledge" or "information" that survives in the ancient German expression "von etwas Wissenschaft haben" (to have knowledge of something). Thus *Wissenschaftslehre* does not mean scientific theory, but the philosophical derivation of human knowledge in general. This was at the same time supposed to satisfy the fundamental preoccupation of modern philosophy, namely the attempt to reorganize modern science back into philosophy, the trustee of the ancient knowledge of mankind. The final attempt to fulfill this task was undertaken by the Romantics. Hegel's speculative synthesis of all the forms in which Spirit appears in art, religion, and philosophy—that is, in intuition, devotion, and thought—was intended to bring together the whole truth.[11] This Romantic dream was soon exhausted. Idealism's speculative synthesis fell before the onslaught of the empirical sciences that were then beginning their triumphant advance. Idealist philosophy of nature became a laughing stock, and the idealist transfiguration of political reality was equally unable to resist. "Progress" became the byword of the new epoch. This inevitably pushed the ideal of theory into the background. Science was supposed to bring universal well-being. The contemplative ideal proved to be only an eschatological dream when, say, Marx saw the true humanism of the future in the abolition (*Aufhebung*) of the division of labor.[12]

From a philosophical point of view, bourgeois nineteenth-century Germany came more and more under Schopenhauer's star. This is one of the most remarkable twists of fate in the history of thought: Arthur Schopenhauer—a child of Goethe's time, that of romantic and idealist reaction against the extremes of the Enlightenment—published his magnum opus, *The World as Will and Representation* as a *Privatdozent* (an unsalaried junior lecturer) in Berlin in 1819. It went unnoticed, only to rise again fifty years later as the fashionable philosophy of the bourgeoisie, to support the cult of Richard Wagner and ultimately to find its literary monument in the story of Buddenbrooks.[13] Schopenhauer saw the same blind and brutish energy of the will at work in both nature and human life, and found reconciliation with this fearful reality in pure meditation (*Betrachtung*), and in the disinterested pleasure (*Wohlgefallen*) in which all will has come to rest. This was an ad lib continuation of Kant's line of thought. He saw redemption from the blind will as brought about through the reconciling power of art. Joining with it, the Indian wisdom that equates the path of health with dissolving all individuality into the All-One[14] comes to complete the ideal of contemplation as release from the pressure of an ever more prosaic reality. This became characteristic of the nineteenth century's concept of art and of its cultural life.

Given the way we have posed our question, this means nothing less than that the liberal era's consciousness of progress, based as it was on science and technology, simply set aside a space for this kind of contemplation to escape into. This could also be accentuated in the consciousness of the individual researchers who had been freed from economic constraints by the public authorities' financial support for science. Once it constituted their profession, researchers could pursue their personal enthusiasm for finding knowledge more than ever. But the process of civilization and the life of society came to be governed more and more by the technological applications of science. So the privilege of pure research, and the self-esteem of theory that went with it, increasingly had to bow to the pressure of political pragmatism. Since the beginning of our century, our highly industrialized society has been proceeding more and more in the direction of applied research. The purely theoretical interests of scientific research have had to assume a more defensive position. This defense has been carried out by distinguishing and honoring it as basic research, necessary for all scientific and technological progress. In the age of the new social utilitarianism that has filled the twentieth century, such research became a modest sanctuary that protected the interests of pure theory without in any way restricting the generally pragmatic perspective. Even when theory is valued in this way, then, it serves the praise of practice. Theory has to justify itself in the forum of practice.

The scientifically shaped cultural consciousness of modernity has certainly gone hand in hand with an increasingly active critique of culture, which intensified still further at the beginning of our century. As alienation from modern labor and cultural life (Bildung) grew, various protest movements appeared, such as the great romantic children's crusade of the youth movement before the First World War, which already marked the threshold of the technocratic age. The full outbreak of this age was the technological slaughter of the First World War. European optimism about progress and bourgeois cultural idealism could not survive this catastrophe. Spengler's vision of the decline of the West perfectly expressed this feeling of shakenness.[15] The idealist concept of the self-realization of Spirit could not remain obligatory, especially as the academic forms of philosophy had not moved beyond variations on the idealist syntheses of Goethe's time. Self-consciousness, that *fundamentum inconcossum* of neo-Kantian Cartesianism,[16] and the epistemology based on it, lapsed into deeper doubt disseminated partly by the era's great romancers, partly by Nietzsche's extreme radicalism, and partly by ideology critique and psychoanalysis.

The eight decades we can survey of our century's world wars and world crises seem strangely unified under this universal aspect, presumably because philosophical consciousness has remained fairly constant since the crisis of the First World War. The consciousness of the time that it reflects has, in the end, persisted to an astonishing extent through all the to and fro of short-term variations. The First World War shattered Europe's self-consciousness. Despite the dissimilarity of their experiences, the two great rising continents of America and Russia should have been made equally sensible of their limits by the Second World War and its consequences. The endangered self-consciousness of our epoch is no longer defined so much by the shifts in these powers' political interrelations or the fundamental dissimilarity of their economic and social systems, as by the inexorable law of progressive industrialization, which applies in the same way to both of them.

The second half of our century has begun to see the spread of this industrialization over the entire globe. We do not know which tensions will drive the global spread of this process until the unequal development of the countries of this earth reaches equilibrium. Nor do we know whether the life-threatening disproportion between the strength of our weapons and the frail wisdom that characterizes the culture of the human race today will plunge humanity into catastrophe and self-destruction. But in any case it is no longer just the romantic critique of culture or the resentful impotence of blind revolt that is undermining faith in progress. The pattern of increasing welfare, rising standards of living, and universal leveling has turned out, on its own terms, to be just as utopian as the moral confidence of the first age of Enlightenment. That confidence was refuted by Rousseau's famous answer to the Dijon Academy's contest question.[17] Today, it seems, there is no need to assert that the future path of humanity depends on things other than technological inventiveness and skill in dealing with the bottlenecks of global industrialization.

All this must be reflected in the philosophical efforts of our century. The primacy of self-consciousness, which must be considered the hallmark of modern philosophy, is closely connected with modern concepts of science and method. For modernity's concept of method is distinguished from ancient ways of understanding and explaining the world precisely by the fact that it represents a way of self-certification. The primacy of self-consciousness is the primacy of method. This should be taken literally: only what can be investigated by method is the object of a science. But this implies that there are marginal cases and gray areas of half-sciences and pseudo-sciences that don't fully satisfy the conditions of scientificity and yet are perhaps not devoid of valuable truth. Moreover, the possibilities of modern science are limited in a far more fundamental way. There will always be areas that fundamentally cannot be approached through objectivization and treated as methodical objects. Many of the things in life are of this kind, and a few gain their unique significance from precisely this fact.

limits of science

For a start, there is the other person, who is just as much an I as I am myself. In philosophy we know this as the transcendental problem of intersubjectivity. How can something that has to find the ultimate proof of its identity in our self-consciousness and is determined as an object of our consciousness in this way, itself be something that is not simply a given object of our perception but is for itself and is itself self-consciousness? This is not just a question of justification that makes problems for transcendental philosophy. Being-for-itself seems to present an ultimate closedness that no systematic observation can break open, a final refusal and an inaccessible otherness. And yet our experience is just the opposite. It is precisely in interpersonal relations that people open themselves up to the kind of intimacy that does not allow me to experience the other as another, as a limit to my own being-with-myself, but rather as an intensification, extension, and restoration of my own particular being, or even as breaking my self-willed obstinacy, and so helping me learn to recognize what is real. What is this intimacy?

intimacy

Or we could take another example, which will then also immediately introduce a problem of modern science. I mean one's own body. The processes that take place in it, on which our health or illness depends, are certainly the object of scientific research; and scientific medicine, rather than practicing an inexplicable healing, is proud to look for ways of influencing them that are based on scientific knowledge, and for treatments that can promise a cure. But again it is still much more than the limit of the doctor's knowledge, which is often quite plain to him, that allows him to encounter the bodiliness of the other as something beyond his perspicuity. The real puzzle is rather that each individual is profoundly intimate with his own body—so intimate that he even finds it disturbing if it comes to his attention at all—and yet it thoroughly conceals itself from the observer. We might ask again what this intimacy is: it is certainly not a higher or a lower form of self-consciousness. And my body is just as little an object for me as is the other person, with whom I am intimate and who is intimate with me.

The examples of intimacy I have chosen are not as arbitrary as they might appear when we consider the unfathomable depths of unreflective intimacy that support us: from the most trivial habits to the magic of home, mother tongue, childhood experience, and so on. These examples have special significance in the context of our inquiry. The intimacy that each of us has with his own body does not just consist in superseding (aufheben) or rendering unremarkable the otherness of the other that the naturalness of our own body represents for our conscious Dasein.[18] Because the body presents itself as something with which we are intimate and not like an obstacle, it is precisely what sets us free and lets us be open for what is. Similarly, we have seen that the individual's immersion in the various kinds of human and social intimacy does more than merely limit the extent to which we can be reduced to objective observers. It is precisely what first teaches us, in our recognition of the other, to recognize reality, and so lets us also acknowledge the reality of far-off times and foreign peoples.

Here we touch the root of what we can call theory: seeing what is. This does not mean merely determining what is in fact present. Even in science, a "fact" is not defined as what is merely present-at-hand that can be fixed by measuring, weighing, and counting; "fact" is rather a hermeneutic concept, which means that it is always referred back to a context of supposition and expectation, to a complicated context of inquiring understanding. What is not quite so complicated, but all the more difficult to achieve, is for each individual in his practical life to see what is, instead of what he would like to be. The fundamental elimination of prejudices that science requires of its researchers may well be a laborious process, but it is always easier than overcoming the illusions that constantly arise from one's own ego (that of an individual, group, people, or culture to which the person belongs and listens) in order to see what is.[19] The secret of all government—the evil of power and its counterpart, the wisdom of political assembly—is hidden here.

It seems helpful to recall here the original Greek sense of theory, *theoria*. The word means observing (the constellations, for example), being an onlooker (at a play, for instance), or a delegate participating in a festival. It does not mean a mere "seeing" that establishes what is present or stores up information. Contemplatio does not dwell on a particular entity, but in a region. Theoria is not so much the individual momentary act as a way of comporting oneself, a position and condition. It is "being present" in the lovely double sense that means that the person is not only present but completely present. Participants in a ritual or ceremony are present in this way when they are engrossed in their participation as such, and this always includes their participating equally with others or possible others. Thus theory is not in the first instance a behavior whereby we control an object or put it at our disposal by explaining it. It has to do with a good of another kind.

There are two essentially very different kinds of goods. The first are those that we try to acquire in order to use them or have them in our possession so that it is possible to use them. It is part of the nature of these goods that what one person possesses and puts to use another person cannot have. These are the goods that are to be distributed, and the efforts of modern government are directed toward distributing them justly. And then there are goods of another kind, whose belonging to one person does not prevent their belonging to others. These actually belong to nobody, and for just that reason they are something in which each individual has a full share. To distinguish the two ways of "having" a good, Augustine used the opposition of *uti* and *frui*, of making use of something and using it up, by contrast to dealing with something in a way that bears its own fruit.[20] What was most important to Augustine was contemplation directed toward God—he condemned the desire for worldly knowledge as curiosity. But all the other ways we resist looking only for the useful and behave "purely theoretically," all the areas we call art and science (but certainly not just those), belong here too. Whenever we find something "beautiful," we don't ask about the why and wherefore of it. Would a human life that failed to participate in this kind of "theory" seem human to us at all?

Is it so romantic to speak of theory as a life force in which all humans have a share? You don't have to be an appointed eulogist of theory to realize that theory is not exhausted by being of immediate service to practice. To be sure, humanity has slowly improved life through a learning process that has taken countless millennia, by constantly making new inventions and developing new capabilities, starting with mastering fire as a weapon, as well as a source of warmth and a beginning of technology. But it is no self-evident matter that theoretical consciousness should have awakened and science should have been developed among the intelligent and inquisitive people of ancient Greece. There are great and mature cultures, not backward in the slightest, that have nevertheless not taken the step to theoretical science.

Isn't there something funny, though, about how someone as sober as Aristotle imagines that theoretical knowledge was first begun? The Greek conviction of the time was that the Egyptians were responsible, since it was there that the caste of priests, freed from having to work for the necessities of life, had the leisure to create idle theories.[21] The pragmatic model suggesting that the superfluous and the beautiful can be nurtured only when the necessities have been provided clearly will not do.

In his *Republic,* Plato showed quite clearly that, as modern civilization is now experiencing so dramatically, the viewpoint of needs and desires opens up a perspective that in itself is unlimited.[22] The condition of happy concord between needs and their satisfaction is not a human condition. For needs grow of their own accord. *Hedone* (desire) belongs to the class of the *apeiron* (limitless).

We do not have to rely on our self-awareness to tell us that the complete satisfaction of human needs cannot be a pre-condition whose fulfillment is necessary before theory is possible. Our historical research also tells us plainly enough — what we experience dramatically in our world — that the viewpoint of needs and desires is of itself unlimited. And yet, as the spadework of research during the early years of this century revealed more about human pre-history, we came to see more clearly that even then we were concerned with more than mere survival. The path of mankind has been attended all along by burial rites; and whatever else they might mean, whatever protest against death or even recognition and acceptance of death they might imply,[23] the consecrations that these tombs bring to light divulge a constantly surprising wealth of super-fluous decorations, and not a confinement to what is necessary. So our more recent theorizing about the history and origins of culture—as illustrated by Aristotle's explanation of the beautiful and the purely theoretical as products of later priestly idle-ness—clearly shows only limited signs of being enlightening.

But in casually construing history in this way, Aristotle really wants to establish something more. Human life desires the "good."[24] Like all living things, man is concerned with his own self-preservation. This thought occurs to him of itself: but he is also a thinker. Each of us asks himself how he should live. He seeks his fulfillment in a happy life—and that is not something that is exhausted by acquiring things and being successful; life is also devoted precisely to what is, to what is to be seen and what is beautiful to see. The great master of those who have since come to know,[25] whose Physics (which is in many ways so false and in many ways so human) held good for two thou-sand years, was the first to develop a practical philosophy that found systematic ideas even in human drives, and was the first to explore the various ways of constituting socio-political life. Nevertheless it was no accommodation to others' beliefs and no lack of consistency that led him to admit the priority of the ideal of the theoretical life.[26] He cannot have meant that some-one could ever have a wholly contemplative life as if he did not remain tied to his own body and embedded in the practical and political relationships from which he must collect what is true and essential. We cannot choose whether to be gods or men—and as men we are not like ever-watchful gods, but are bodily natural creatures. As men we are also always men among men, social creatures, and it is only from within human practice that one person or another can turn for a while toward pure knowledge from time to time.

Could this solve the old problem of Aristotelian theology—that God's "thinking" cannot think anything but itself, although thinking must still always be thinking of something and only "additionally" directed to itself as well?[27] If *noein* is *theorein*,[28] there is no meaningful question as to what the object of this contemplation can be: for us, the highest fulfillment of our "there" is the "how" of being abandoned to what is, not a "self-consciousness," but just that intensification of living that the Greeks called theoria. For them, the divine consisted in precisely the lasting present of this intensification.

It would not be hard to show that modern science always presupposes this concept of theory as a condition of its own existence. But where does that get us? In returning to the basic constitution of mankind, are we actually still dealing with theory, or with practice and interactions between people and things that we certainly could not call theoretical? Can this be right? Is theory ultimately a practice, as Aristotle already stressed,[29] or is practice, if it is truly human practice, always at the same time theory? Is it not, if it is human, a looking away from oneself and looking out toward the other, disregarding oneself and listening for the other? Life, then, is a unity of theory and practice that is the possibility and the duty of everyone. Disregarding oneself, regarding what is: that is the behavior of a cultivated, I might almost say a divine, consciousness. It does not need to be a consciousness cultivated by and for science; it only needs to be a humanly cultivated consciousness that has learned to think along with the viewpoint of the other and try to come to an understanding about what is meant and what is held in common.

But what has happened to our praise of theory, then? Has it become a praise of practice? Just as the individual who needs relevant knowledge must constantly reintegrate theoretical knowledge into the practical knowledge of his everyday life, so also a culture based on science cannot survive unless rationalizing the apparatus of civilization is not an end in itself, but makes possible a life to which one can say "yes." In the end, all practice suggests what points beyond it.

3

The Power of Reason

The underlying conviction of all kinds of enlightenment is a faith in reason and in its triumphant power. What we today call "philosophy" is understood as bringing about such enlightenment. This is the case not only in the West, where something we now call "science" has been developed in a double movement: the Greeks' overcoming mythological consciousness on the one hand, and on the other, emancipation from the pressures of authoritarian medieval church doctrine. Even extra-European cultures, old and young, reflect the appropriation of modern science in European thinking, whether one views the positivism of scientific theory, economic materialism, or the idealism of freedom as the real secret of modern civilization. If philosophy were really the true science of reason, or the reason of science, then there would be no doubt that reason in the shape of Philosophy could today justly resume the truly dominant position in human life that she used to possess as queen of the sciences.

But in fact it hardly seems meaningful to ask whether reason has power any more, when what all human experience expresses is precisely the impotence of reason: the power of passion that can ravish an individual despite all his rational intentions; the might of economic, social, and political power-interests that prevail against all constitutional, democratic, or socialist principles; the madness of destructive wars in which one people is incited against another (as though war could ever be a lesser evil in comparison to some other greater); and now as the final

A speech given in Vienna, 2 September 1968.

consequence of the victory of modern science, we have the breathtaking specter of all mankind's self-destruction through misuse of atomic energy.

Yet not only can the thinker discern behind the obvious impotence of human reason everybody's hope and trust that in the end reason will still win the day. Not only does he hope that as individuals continue to turn to reason it might bring about great forms of rational compromise in human life. He also has reasons to believe so. It may be difficult to recognize what is rational as long as our own interests fixate us blindly on what is closest, but people still unite when they are faced with obvious unreason. All we have to do is make what is unreasonable stand out as such. If we do so successfully, then reason, wherever it is brought to words, develops an irresistible power. What are the conditions under which it can exhibit this power? Where can we find them? How can we produce them?

At this point, it seems, the plot thickens. It all comes down to the fact that the conditions under which we could speak of reason in all things seem rather utopian. So we must ask ourselves how it ever comes about that reason is actually brought to words. Reason obviously makes an immediate reference to the universal. When nothing holds sway as reason, it is continually necessary to gain everyone's consent. This can be seen most clearly in the sciences that deal with the pure objects of reason: mathematics and logic. Their objects exhibit the rational procedures that produced them, which makes their irrefutable truth plain, and the same is the case wherever reason exercises such self-governance. Sometimes this can even lead to surprising implications, as when, for instance, we are dealing with the decidability of propositions or the mutual compatibility of independently rationally derived propositions. But it is incontestable that only reason and nothing else can be of further assistance here.

Now these are admittedly examples of sciences of pure reason. But since the Enlightenment ideal of gaining new knowledge of the world by means of pure reason and conceptual analysis was rendered untenable by Hume's skepticism and by Kant's Critique of Pure Reason, "science" has come to mean not so much "science of reason" as "science of experience." It may be that our reason keeps clinging to the idea of recognizing "reason" in the organization of the world as the goal of all research, but it does not expect any success except through the process of experience, and the progress of individual research. The very idea that there could be reason in history, that the course of human affairs could still satisfy the demands of reason once it is no longer read as a divine story of religious promise and hope, seems wholly illegitimate as a regulative idea, even to historical research itself: to this extent the standpoint of experience, and especially of the historical experience that mankind has had of itself, has discredited faith in reason.

And yet the whole of our modern faith in science remains indirect evidence of the power of reason, and one does well to be aware of both the value and the limitations of this evidence. The old faith that human reason is a copy or image, a piece or seed of God's infinite reason that controls the making and course of the world, does not of itself legitimize modern science and its discoveries. It seems, rather, to be the other way round: it is the ingenuity of scientists that provides no trifling evidence of the power of reason. For the development of science confronts each and every man with the limits of his own reason and his own capacity for judgment. So it is our being educated in science, above all, that now makes us critical of hearsay and restricts the know-all's naïve analogies based on particular experiences. But does the existence of science in this sense guarantee the victory of reason?

The fathers of Western culture, the Greeks, not only created science—geometry, astronomy, medicine, biology, and politics —they also saw how extraordinary it is that science is possible for human beings. Plato invented a whole ideal state in order to demonstrate, in its utopian organizations and arrangements, what a huge and almost superhuman task it is for people to direct their thinking beyond their own immediate advantage— and he specified education in the sciences, mathematics, music, and astronomy as the path to this goal. And Aristotle, in addition, soberly analyzed the connection that exists between the human capacity for theoretical interests and the way education in the family and the social system forms human beings. Devoting oneself entirely to "theoretical pursuits" presupposes "practical knowledge"—the guiding force of reason in human action and behavior. This is what really constitutes "reason," its power or its impotence. It is not simply a faculty one has, but something to be cultivated, and its cultivation should serve that political science which, as "scientia practica sive politica,"[1] has cooperated with the self-governance of practical reason in various historically changing forms, right down to the centuries of modern science. As a practical knowledge of practical reason, it teaches us the conditions under which reason becomes practical. It points out the forces that derive from the very fact that we live together as people, without thereby limiting reason's critical capacity for distinguishing the better from the worse. For this practical reason is certainly not, as Aristotle of course occasionally has it,[2] limited to just the means of bringing about given ends. It is not some practical sense that always finds the right means and the right way to whatever end is being sought. On the contrary, "rationality" (*Vernünftigkeit*) is a way of holding oneself, which one holds onto and which holds one, so as to keep on re-creating and protecting the moral and human order that is established in common norms.[3] In Aristotle the talk is only of means to an end because identification with the communal, with what is best in general, is already presupposed before any action is considered. Precisely because "practical reason" is always at the same time concerned with concretizing what might fulfill the meaning of life, with what forms *eudaimonia*, the unity of "practical science" maintains itself through all kinds of changes in social relationships—from the ancient slave society through the Christian feudalism of the Middle Ages, the bourgeois constitution of city guilds, the formation of the modern civic state amid sovereign governments and the emancipation of the "tiers état" (third estate), right up to our own day. Only as the idea of science began to be completely subordinated to the self-understanding of modern natural science, to its idea of method and its demand for verification, has the knowledge intrinsic to this "practical science" been deprived more and more of its legitimacy.

Now, what modern science has brought humankind is really something quite extraordinary: the domination of nature on a whole new scale and in a whole new sense. For the methodical procedure that had its first great successes in Galileo's and Huygens' mechanics[4] and found its philosophical expression in Descartes' concept of method[5] fundamentally altered the relationship between theory and practice. Human practice, with all its possibilities for dominating nature and for inventing and making necessary and beautiful things, no longer saw itself as restricted to filling areas that nature had left open for it; and theoria, knowledge about the natural order of things, could no longer be seen as "above all of that" on the grounds that it deals with what is beautiful and so serves no end. By means of abstraction, measurement, and calculation, the new knowledge penetrated the laws that control nature, isolated the part that each individual factor played in the result and so, wherever it was successful, disclosed conditions that man himself had the power to alter, so that people could bring about the results they wanted. Although the new science was directed as exclusively as ever toward finding out about nature—deciphering its mysteries with wonder and discovering the laws that order it, which leave all human forms of law and order infinitely far behind them—it now consisted in knowing various possibilities for governing natural processes, and it therefore of itself entered the boundlessly expanding realm of human practice.

The course of research that revealed pre-eminently the construction of matter, and with it the possibilities for materially transforming the givens of nature (Francis Bacon's ideal), was certainly a laborious one. At first it was only the lowest levels of the material and economic substructure of the realms of social practice that were altered and enriched. But when the ways in which human society is organized were subordinated to human reason, it certainly marked no categorical change in the knowledge involved in planning and construction that had had such immense success in controlling nature. For me it is the very signature of our epoch that, after the persistence of precedent held us back for so long, a real attempt is being made to ground the organization of society on the discoveries of empirical science. Does the completion of this undertaking perhaps signal the definitive victory of reason? Is the much-decried impotence of reason with respect to the passions and the interests of individuals and groups in the end just a vestige left behind in a rationally administered world, which we should be able to eliminate rationally through individual psychology, social economics, and scientific politics?

Perhaps it is this trust that prevents people from being upset by the fact that the Eastern and Western forms of social organization are today so sharply opposed to one another. After all, it might always turn out that after countless setbacks, attempts to impose a solution by force, repressions, and regressions, the inevitable demands of rational obligation (*rationale Sachzwang*) will come ever more dominantly into force in both East and West and will bring in changes in both places that will weaken the opposition between the world-views, social conditions, and forms of government, and ultimately end in the equilibrium of a perfectly administered world that nothing further will be able to disturb. Is this the power of reason in which we trust? And are we, as philosophers, sworn to this ideal?

However optimistic one is and however little a skeptic, one can still be a little dubious about all this. Old Platonic strains force themselves upon the ear: science that transforms itself into practice; ability that, because it can, also *must*, always developing new abilities that reach further and further—is this what reason consists in? Plato once had his Socrates remind a young admirer of the new sophistic art of discourse and argumentation about bodily nourishment: the cook's flattering art cannot succeed against the rational advice of the doctor—and it is especially necessary in the case of spiritual nourishment that one have enough reason to judge how wholesome it is.[6] Indeed, reason would be in control only when what can be done is not as good as done already, just because it can be done. Now, in modern industrial society the reason that guides what can be done is surely always at work, whether as the commercial reason of the producer assessing the market or the planner assessing demand and setting the priorities for satisfying it or whatever. And all of them will make use of scientific advice in their planning, just like the officials who administer public matters, including so-called culture politics. After all, it is not only in business, or wherever economic questions come into play, that people turn to scientific rationality. Rather, it is altogether characteristic of an age that typically converts science into practice that science commands attention whenever it has something to say. A good example of this is the role played by so-called experts in the modern judicial system. A court, in trying its cases, is scarcely permitted to exercise its right to pronounce sentence in the absence of or contrary to expert opinion.[7]

Now we do know that the specialization of modern research necessarily produces a specific kind of blindness, because specialists can see only what is accessible to their own particular methods. This is known, and science is becoming ever more aware of it and takes it into account by making the phenomena marginal to one discipline, falling outside its methodological competence, the central focus of another, new discipline of systematic research, trying in this way to combat the dangers of specialization; and widely diverse research orientations concerning an object can often be fruitfully integrated. All this seems no more than reasonable.

But Plato draws his ingenious picture with more and different things in mind than this. He is not recommending the doctor's dietary authority as a model for rationally monitoring cultural politics and subjecting it to state censorship (like the critique of poetry caricatured in the *Statesman*).[8] On the contrary, he is emphasizing how incompatible is "spiritual nourishment" with the way it is proffered to people by the new rhetoric. For this nourishment—that of convictions imparted through speech—cannot be tested before it is brought to table, but instead goes straight in, and anyone who listens to these ideas and allows himself to be talked into them has already been taken in by them. This is the danger that attends all "speaking" (*Reden*) whether in education and training or in public life. What possesses us in this way makes us prepossessed. Now, no human community is possible without the power of convincing speech that reaches everybody, and the new rhetoric of the modern mass media is actually similar to the sophistic paideia of fifth century Athens, and even exceeds it because the technological form of its dissemination no longer offers the listener or reader any speaker on the other side to whom one could oneself address one's own words: this new rhetoric, just like the old kind, forestalls all critical consideration and summons the power of the self-evident. Everything that is self-evident, that has become self-evident or has been stated persuasively until it achieves self-evidence, necessarily pre-determines even methodical research, its choice of how to frame its questions and the evaluation of its results. The judgments of expert witnesses who answer in court for their results, as well as the public that accepts them, are even more affected and restricted in this way. We call these prior determinants of our judgment our prejudices. Now the Enlightenment wanted to strive against all prejudices: freedom from prejudice, the Enlightenment slogan, found the concretization of its theory in the ideal of presuppositionless science. Wasn't that the final victory of Enlightenment? A real victory?

It is true that the fundamental and essential law of science is to leave no prejudice untested, to subject all phenomena that are not understood or cannot yet be controlled to a theoretical investigation so that science can master them. The objection that specialized scientific methodology is just as subject to the new rhetoric (today called the formation of public opinion) as the public sphere itself is certainly not valid for genuine research without further ado. But it has nothing at all to do with what results the researcher himself gets from his research, but only how these results enter the public consciousness. And precisely because this is the decisive point, the new Enlightenment, like the old rhetoric, has taken this as its starting point. The formation of public opinion rightly plays a significant role in the new science of society, and scientific research is trying to devise scientific means of guiding opinion formation. Increasingly, specialists in opinion formation—opinion pollsters, advertisers, sociologists, social psychologists, and political analysts—are extending the circle of scientists whose judgment counts. None of them, to be sure, can avoid the rules and procedures of modern science, especially if they take their responsibility as men of science seriously. The law of specialization rules over everybody in this way. The efforts of the social researcher are aimed at controlling the objects they study and overcoming their resistance to that research—but that means they make them usable for any ends we please. It is in the nature of the thing: the real public responsibility of science that has troubled the researcher's conscience since Hiroshima cannot be borne by any science as such. Scientific reason is not the reason that serves the classical *scientia practica et politica*.

This has its immediate expression in what I might call the incomprehensibility of science. This has existed all along, and to a greater degree since higher mathematics became indispensable for modern measuring and manufacturing. But it passed completely into the public consciousness and had public consequences only when the modern social sciences began to control social practice. For this has made identifying with the universal—and what else is reason?—into the most burning problem of our social life. How is this supposed to succeed when a politics of public opinion formation brings to bear scientific judgment, which resists critical examination by laymen, against the formation of any individual judgment? Does genuine participation in socio-political life that reaches beyond specialized vocational training not become impossible when all communication is targeted at the formation of particular opinions, and obligations have everywhere been brought into effect that necessitate things' being as they are and not otherwise? Here lies the root of the suspicion of the establishment harbored by young people.

But we all witness it. Experiences come to words in language common to us all, in new words that enter common usage. There are two words in particular—one of them young, the other, although older, embracing an almost limitless realm—

which even just in the way they are formed betray how much we all feel a loss of freedom and the impossibility of identifying with the universal: "technocracy" and "bureaucracy." Clearly, both word-forms are modeled on the word "autocracy"—in any case they share with the word "autocracy" (and not with similar words like "aristocracy" or "democracy") the stigma of impotence in the face of superior potency, and this not just in the sense in which all rational obligation restricts and debilitates one's own will. For what both these words express is the need to look at things rationally and identify with one's own insight. Just as the will of an autocrat makes all identification with universal interests impossible because he is not bound by the universal of law and justice (eighteenth-century juridical hermeneutics was explicitly limited by the will of the overlord), so someone who is seen as a technocrat is the representative of an alien power inaccessible to reason. He remains a challenge to both the individual and social need to be rational, even if no one doubts that his plans and intentions are backed by the reason of science and if he is an expert on the whole apparatus of public opinion formation. Reason may tell us that the planner of new things necessarily stands in tension with the status quo—think of, say, town planning instigated by architects— but this kind of insight cannot bridge the gap between the experts and the reason or unreason of laymen.

And, finally, "bureaucracy," acknowledged as the basic evil in the rational administration of the world, bemoaned and resisted under every form of modern state and yet still making lively progress for apparently inescapable material reasons, this oldest insult hurled by peasants and commoners at the governors and authorities, attacks, in the name of a reason attempting to be common and universal, not only the unintelligibility but the unintelligence of administrative activities. Their scorn thus conceived defends the last bastions of a common reason, the

reason Heraclitus demanded we should follow, and for which—
as what is commonly held to apply, as the *nomoi*—he urged us
to strive still more valiantly than for the walls of the city.[9]

Or is the situation of reason, of actually identifying with the
universal, not so hopeless after all? Don't worry that I'm going
to conclude by recommending philosophers as the experts of
reason, so that the power of reason can finally be raised beyond
all doubt by filling our panel of experts. We should be careful not to make fools of ourselves, especially by claiming that
our specialty is the universal that is reason: let alone that reason should come to power through us. But perhaps it is, all in
all, a contradiction in terms that reason should have power and
exercise governance, and perhaps it is quite in order that the
strange guild of philosophers should remain almost invisible in
the real power struggles between peoples, states, classes, religions, world-views, and economic systems. We do not speak in
the name of reason. Anyone who speaks in the name of reason contradicts himself. For it is reasonable to acknowledge
that one's own insight is limited and for just that reason to be
capable of better insights, wherever they may come from.

To be sure, this definition is so universal that it applies equally
to scientific reason insofar as every researcher always knows that
he can himself be surpassed. But for just this reason science
persists in its ways. It is nevertheless reasonable, as we saw, to
be aware that science is limited by its inability to reflect on its
own presuppositions and consequences. This too is an insight
that overcomes a prejudice, just like when an individual cor-
rects old prejudices with a new insight. Reason always consists
in not blindly insisting on what one holds true, but engaging
critically with it. This is still what enlightenment does, but not
in the dogmatic form of a new absolute rationality (Rationalität) that always knows better—reason also needs to be grasped

with respect to itself and its own contingency in a process of constant self-enlightenment.

The words that Symmachus, an honorable heir of ancient culture, directed on behalf of ancient Roman tradition against the new religion's claim to power, still speak today in the name of reason against all dogmatism wherever it may arise:

Uno itinere non potest perveniri ad tam grande secretum.[10]
We cannot arrive at such a great secret by one path alone.

4

The Ideal of Practical Philosophy

The problems of practical reason arise in many areas but primarily, in my opinion, with respect to the self-understanding of the human sciences.[1] What position do the humanities, the *Geisteswissenschaften*, occupy in the scientific cosmos? [I shall try to show that the only productive or appropriate way for the human sciences to think of themselves is on the model of Aristotle's practical philosophy rather than the modern concept of scientific method. I shall lead into this provocative thesis with a short historical summary of the situation.]

When the ancient Greeks discovered the concept of science, this was the true turning point when what we call Western culture was born: science is the glory of our culture but perhaps also, if we compare it with the great cultures of Asia, its undoing. For the Greeks, science was essentially represented by mathematics—the genuine, and the only, science of reason. Mathematics deals with what is unchangeable, and only where something is unchangeable can we have knowledge of it without having to take another look from time to time.

In one way, modern science has had to retain this axiom in order to understand itself as science at all. The unchangeable laws of nature have taken the place of what constituted the main content of mathematically inspired Greek wisdom, the

An essay published in 1980 as Vom Ideal der praktischen Philosophie in *Universitas* 35, pp. 623–630. Passages in square brackets are taken from a longer version of this essay entitled "Problems of Practical Reason," also published in 1980: Probleme der praktischen Vernunft in *Sinn und Geschichtlichkeit* Klett-Cotta, Stuttgart, pp. 147–156.

Pythagorean science of the numbers and the stars. It is clear that on this model, human affairs hold little promise of being knowable. Morals and politics, the laws that men set up, the values by which they live, the institutions they create, and the habits they follow—none of these can lay claim to being unchangeable or therefore genuinely knowable.

From the point of view of modern science, of course, the ancient heritage of scientific thought has been re-established on a new basis: a new epoch of knowledge of the world began with Galileo. From that point on, the object of scientific questioning has been determined by a new conception of knowability. This is the concept of method, and its primacy over the subject matter: the objects of science are defined by the conditions of methodical knowability. This raises the question of what kind of science the *humaniora* (that peculiar comparative that always makes one ask what the superlative, a truly human science, would really look like), these sciences of human affairs that we call the Geisteswissenschaften, could be under these circumstances.

To a great extent they obviously follow modern scientific thinking. But at the same time they carry on the old tradition of human knowledge that has characterized the history of Western culture (*Bildungsgeschichte*) since antiquity. [Even John Stewart Mill, the famous author of *Inductive Logic*,[2] a book that determined how the science that blossomed in the nineteenth and twentieth centuries originally understood itself, used the ancient name for the Geisteswissenschaften in calling them the "moral sciences." But for Mill (and I'm not joking) they had the same scientific status as meteorology: their statements were thought as reliable as those of long-range weather forecasting. This is patently extrapolated from a concept of empirical science modeled on the success of the modern natural sciences.] Since then it has become one of the tasks of philosophy to uphold the autonomous validity of the "human" sciences, the humaniora.

There used to be no need for this. Rhetoric was the current of uncontested tradition that bore man's ancient knowledge of man. [This sounds a little strange to modern ears, as we think of "rhetoric" as a pejorative term for irrelevant argument. But we should restore the true breadth of the concept. It includes every spoken form of communication and is what holds human society together. There would be no human society if we could not speak to and understand one another without resorting to logical arguments. So it's worth reminding ourselves of the significance of rhetoric and its place in modern science.

It's plain that rhetoric in the Greek sense never counted as science. But it's just as plain that in the eyes of a Greek thinker historical writings, for example, were not scientific either. They both belong in the same great domain of speaking and writing well. When Sextus Empiricus questioned the value of the sciences in his famous skeptical arguments[3] it certainly never occurred to him to say a single word about history.] So we have a new question: how does our civilization — characterized as it is by science, that is, by modern empirical science — represent the heritage of ancient rhetoric and the opportunity it offers to justify and found scientifically the knowledge of man it has bequeathed to us?

[To demonstrate this fully, I might point out how the historian's ideal changed between the eighteenth and nineteenth centuries. It changed from Plutarch, the late Greek author who presented the eighteenth century with a great drama of moral experience in his parallel biographies of great men, the Vitae parallelae,[4] to Thucydides,[5] that other great — in a sense even greater — Greek historian who ranks as the foremost hero of modern critical history thanks to his critical attitude to the reports of his contemporaries, his careful scrutiny of eye-witnesses' prejudices, and especially his almost superhuman impartiality.

Now my question is how the new critical scientific understanding fits in with the old understanding that people develop for, among and along with other people.] To put this question in a modern way: what is the epistemological character of the so-called human sciences? Are they really just inexact sciences that might compete at best with long-range weather forecasting, or do they have some privilege that mathematics, the most exact of all sciences (by which I mean of course that it is the only science of pure reason), perhaps does not itself possess? The epistemological problem can also be formulated in terms of the relationship of fact to theory. As such it is a universal problem: providing a critical justification of ourselves as men of science.

This problem is not confined to the human sciences. It is clear that even in the natural sciences, it is theory that really determines and confirms the actual epistemic value of established facts. The mere accumulation of facts constitutes no experience at all, let alone the foundation of empirical science. It is the "hermeneutic" relationship between fact and theory that is decisive in this field too. [The Vienna School's epistemological attempts to erect natural science on the basis that observation statements are indubitably certain because of the direct simultaneity of the observer and the observed was already refuted, decisively I think, by Moritz Schlick in the earliest stages of the Vienna Circle (1934).][6]

Nonetheless, if we concern ourselves only with this "hermeneutic" critique of facts from the point of view of their forming theories, we shall only do justice to the human sciences to a minimal degree. For in the end only Max Weber's grand, though somewhat quixotic, enterprise[7] remains to extend "value-free science" to knowledge of society. The field in which the genuine hermeneutic problem[8] presents itself is that of the knowledge of man and of man's knowledge about himself, not just that of isolating the reciprocal relationship of theory and fact.

In the late nineteenth century, with the increasing dominance of the south-west German school (which Max Weber followed to a certain extent), the key principle was that the human sciences could establish themselves on the definition of a historical fact. It is clear that a historical fact is not simply a fact and that not everything that happens can be called a historical fact. What elevates a fact into a historical fact? The familiar answer is the reference to values: it signifies something in the course of things that Napoleon caught a cold at the battle of Wagram (or wherever it was). Not all the colds people catch are historical facts. So the theory of values was the dominant theory. But there is no science of values. Thus Max Weber came to the radical conclusion that questions of value ought to be eliminated from science altogether and that sociology must look for a new basis.

Now this Neo-Kantian philosophy of history was certainly a slender basis for a theory of values. The romantic heritage of the German spirit—the heritage of Hegel and of Friedrich Schleiermacher that came to be disseminated principally through Wilhelm Dilthey's efforts to find a hermeneutic foundation for the human sciences—should have proved more influential. Dilthey's thinking was broader than Neo-Kantian epistemology, for he took over Hegel's full legacy—the doctrine of objective spirit. This doctrine holds that spirit finds its embodiment not only in subjectivity but also in the objectification of institutions, systems of behavior, and systems of life as economy, justice, and society, respectively, and so comes to be an object of possible understanding as "culture."[9] Of course, Dilthey's attempt to revive Schleiermacher's hermeneutics[10] and so to base the humaniora on the identity between the understander and the understood, was doomed to failure insofar as history involves a much deeper strangeness and alienness than what could be seen so confidently from the standpoint of its intelligibility. [Dilthey's model of historical understanding is autobiography—the case where someone has lived through historical events and looks back to interpret what he has seen with his own eyes; this detail is a characteristic symptom of his overlooking the "facticity" of events. Autobiography is always much more like a story of private illusions than the understanding of real historical events.]

On the other hand, the limits of history of ideas, this idealist or spiritual-historical identification of spirit and history, were discovered with the change ushered in by the twentieth century, for which, I personally believe, Husserl and Heidegger were decisively responsible. In Husserl's later work the magic word *Lebenswelt* (life-world) appears [11]—one of those rare and wonderful artificial words (it does not appear before Husserl) that have found their way into the general linguistic consciousness, thus attesting to the fact that they bring an unrecognized or forgotten truth to language. So the word "Lebenswelt" has reminded us of the presuppositions that underlie all scientific knowledge.

Heidegger's program of a "hermeneutics of facticity" [12] (which means confronting the intrinsic incomprehensibility of factical Dasein) was a complete break with idealist hermeneutics. Understanding and wanting to understand were recognized as being in tension with what really happens. Both Husserl's doctrine of the life-world and Heidegger's concept of the hermeneutics of facticity stress the temporality and finitude of man against the unending task of understanding and truth.

Now it is my thesis that this insight shows us that knowledge need not just boil down to the question of how we can dominate what is other and alien: yet that is the basic feeling of the scientific investigation of reality still alive in our natural sciences (perhaps also because of a last faith in the rationality of the world). I claim that, on the contrary, it is not objectivity (*Objektivität*) that is essential in the "human sciences," but the prior relation to their objects (*Gegenstände*). In this realm of knowledge I would supplement the ideal of objective knowledge erected by the ethos of science with the ideal of participation. The real criterion for whether or not the human sciences have any content is whether or not they participate in the essential expressions of human experience formulated in art and history. In my work I have tried to show that the model of dialogue is significant because it illuminates the structure of this form of participation. For dialogue is distinguished by the fact that no one participant can survey what comes out of it and then claim that he can master the subject on his own, but instead that we share together in the truth and in one another.

[I have explained all of this to give credibility to the significance of Aristotle's practical philosophy and the tradition it began. In the end it will provide a common ground beneath rhetoric and critical thinking, between the traditional form of man's self-knowledge and modern science's reduction of everything to alien objectivity.] Aristotle developed practical philosophy, which includes politics, in express opposition to the ideal of theory and theoretical philosophy. In doing so he raised human practice into an independent domain of knowledge. "Praxis" signifies all things practical, including all human behavior and all the ways people organize themselves in this world, not least of which is politics and, within that, legislation. ["Constitution" in the broadest sense, the self-regulation of the social and political order, is the main problem whose solution rules and orders human affairs.]

So what is the theoretical status of the desire to know and reflect about practice and about politics? Aristotle occasionally mentions a threefold division of *philosophia* into theoretical, practical and poetical philosophy[13] (within this third group the famous Poetics has come down to us, and rhetoric, the making of speeches, belongs to it too). But practice, the object of practical philosophy, stands between the two extremes of knowing and doing or creating. Its real basis is clearly man's central position and distinctive nature, the fact that he leads his own life not by following instinctive compulsions but with reason. Thus, the basic virtue that stems from the nature of man is the rationality (*Vernünftigkeit*) that guides his practice.

The Greek expression for this is *phronesis*. Aristotle asks how practical rationality is situated between the scientists' self-consciousness and that of the doers, makers, engineers, technicians, artisans, etc. How is the virtue of rationality situated alongside and together with the virtue of being scientific and the virtue of being technically adept? [Even knowing nothing about Aristotle, one can immediately recognize that this practical rationality must have a superior position. What would come of our place in life and our own affairs if the expert reigned supreme and the technocrat had free rein? Do we not have to make our own moral and political decisions? But this also means that the only way we can feel as politically responsible as when each individual answers for himself is when the decision is taken by a rational and responsible politician in whom we place our trust.]

Aristotle's practical philosophy depends on this question, which is personified by Socrates. An account must be given of what kind of claim this kind of rationality or responsibility has, and this is what philosophy is about, which means that it demands conceptual endeavor. One has to grasp the reason for the fact that alongside theory, alongside the all-consuming passion to know (which has its anthropological basis in the primitive fact of curiosity) there is another genuinely all-encompassing use of reason that consists not in a learnable skill or in blind conformism but in one's rational responsibility to oneself.

One crucial idea runs through both the so-called human sciences and "practical philosophy:" in both, the fundamentally finite constitution of man [14] takes on a decisive role with respect to the infinite task of knowing. This is obviously the essential way to characterize what we call rationality (Vernünftigkeit), or what we mean by someone's being reasonable: that he has overcome the temptation of dogmatism that goes with all supposed knowledge. So someone can strive for what he wants and try to bring it about through his actions, but he must always find his ground in the givens of our finite Dasein. [Aristotle formulates this by saying that the principle of practical matters is the "that," the *"hoti."*[15] This is no mystical wisdom. In terms of the philosophy of science, it simply makes explicit that the underlying principle here is fact.]

How can factuality take on the character of a principle, of the primary and definitive starting point? Here, "fact" does not refer to the factuality of a strange fact that one copes with by learning how to account for it. It is the factuality (*Tatsächlichkeit*) of the convictions, values, and habits that we all share with the deepest inner clarity and the most profound communality, the quintessence of all that goes to make up our way of life. The Greek word for this quintessential factuality is the well known concept of *ethos,* the being that comes about through practice and habituation.[16] Aristotle is the founder of ethics because he privileged this factuality as the definitive kind. Phronesis, answerable rationality, can ensure that this ethos is not mere indoctrination or accession to custom and has nothing to do with the conformism of a half-guilty conscience (but note that it only ensures this where people actually possess this rationality (Vernünftigkeit); it is no gift of nature.) That we come to know ourselves by exchanging ideas with our fellow men, by living together in society and in the state, that we come to common convictions and decisions, is certainly not conformism. On the contrary, it constitutes the very dignity of being a self and of self-understanding. [Anyone who is not "asocial" has always already accepted others, the exchange of ideas and the construction of a common world of convention.

"Convention" is something better than the word's contemporary connotations might suggest. It means agreement that has currency—not a mere externally prescribed system of rules but the identity between an individual's consciousness and convictions represented in other people's consciousness, between the various ways we organize our lives. In one sense, this is a question of rationality, but not just in the sense of pragmatic and technological reason in which we generally use the word when we say, "If I want such and such, a rational first step is to do such and such." That is Max Weber's famous means-end rationality.[17] If we want a particular end, we are obliged to know which means serve this end and which do not. So ethics is not just a matter of principles. We must also answer for our knowledge or our lack of it. Knowledge is a part of "ethos." But rationality, in the great moral and political sense of Aristotelian phronesis, without doubt goes beyond knowing how to use the right means for given ends.] In human society, everything depends on how that society sets its goals or, better still, on how it gets everybody to agree on the goals that they affirm and finds the right means to achieve them. Now it seems crucially important for understanding the desire for theoretical knowledge in the domain of human practical life that in every case, prior to all theoretical justification, we presuppose a previous commitment to an ideal of rationality with determinate content.

[A science with contentful presuppositions! This is the kind of problem in the philosophy of science with which the discussion of practical philosophy really belongs. Aristotle thought about this when he said, for example, "Before we can learn anything about practical philosophy or about conceiving norms for human behavior or the rational constitution of a state, we must first be educated and so become capable of rationality."[18] Here, "theory" presupposes "participation." These are ideas that Kant also meticulously developed in a quite different context: if we think of rationality as a human moral quality independent of theoretical capabilities, how can we still tolerate a theory or philosophy of morals at all? There is a famous note in Kant's notebooks where he says, "Rousseau has set me right!" What he means is that he learned from Rousseau that the perfection of civilization and the zenith of intellectual culture are no guarantee of progress for human morality. He went on to build his famous moral philosophy on this deep insight. Human moral self-justification is a job for morality itself, not for philosophy. Kant's often invoked "categorical imperative" was no more than the abstract formulation of what everyone's "practical" responsibility to himself tells him. It invokes the acknowledgment that no kind of knowledge based on reason can claim any kind of superiority over the practical autonomy of our rationality. Practical philosophy itself depends on practical conditions. Its principle is the "that." In Kantian language this is called "formalism" in ethics.]

This ideal of practical philosophy is valid for the human sciences, even if they do not realize it. [They are not called the "moral sciences" for nothing. They illuminate not a particular domain of objects, but the quintessence of humanity's self-objectification, our doing and suffering as well as our lasting creations.] For the practical universality implied by the concept of rationality (Vernünftigkeit)[(or the lack of it)] comprehends us all through and through. Thus, for theoretical knowledge, which as such acknowledges no limitations, it represents the supreme authority to which theory is answerable, in both the social and the natural sciences. This is the implication of Aristotle's "practical philosophy," which he also calls politics. Reason demands the proper application of knowledge and ability[19] —and this application always involves submitting at the same time to the common ends that apply to us all. The communality of these ends has begun more and more to encompass the whole of humanity. If that is the case, then hermeneutics as the theory of application—that is, of bringing the universal and the individual together—is in fact a central philosophical task. Not only does it have to mediate between universal theoretical knowledge and practical knowledge, it must also see whether the ends to which we put our abilities measure up to the common ends that support our own cultutre and that of humanity in general. Consequently, hermeneutics holds sway not only in science but throughout the whole breadth of human understanding.

5

Science and the Public Sphere

The Enlightenment axiom "Dare to make use of your own reason" inaugurated modern scientific culture. Ever since Wilhelm von Humboldt's reform of university politics,[1] the *universitas* of research and teaching has been the hallmark of the German university. It is the foundation of the new *absolutum* of science. Since then, scientificity is a value to which everyone—theologians as well as lawyers and doctors—gives priority over their own standards. Since then the whole weight of the unity of research and teaching is evident in our job titles and the prosaic distinctions we draw nowadays: the *Naturwissenschaftler* (natural scientist) on one side, the *Geisteswissenschaftler* (human scientist) on the other. These terms often characterize people's functions in the economy, the administration, the educational system, and other areas of social life. The researcher, the scientist, is no longer someone allowed by the indulgence of people in power to administer cultural goods: he has become the expert. In the age of a third Enlightenment, the appeal to experts and especially to social experts, and the whole model of applying the natural sciences to the tasks of modern mass society—all this has given the absolutum of scientificity a whole new explosive effect.

We can see the internal interweaving, and we see the state's mounting dependency on science, which obliges it to take science more and more under its own protection and oversight. And on the other side we have science's mounting dependence on the modern state. In a thoroughly rationalized political sys-

A lecture given in Marburg in 1977.

tem that leaves no space free of political responsibility, science insists on maintaining the freedom of theory and research. It insists on maintaining research, and this in the interests of the economic system. But everyone knows that in recent decades the mounting costs of doing so have spurred mounting expectations on the part of the state. And the third thing we see is an after-effect: worry about our cultural standards, worry about the public sphere itself, worry about the state. This is where we see emerging all the problems in the educational system that have recently developed precisely out of the state's interest in preparing us well, from our earliest youth, for professional life, as well as the problems of universities that have reduced the free space of research by requiring increased teaching. In this situation, the conflict between the claim of science and the claim of society becomes a pressing object for reflection.

The conflict between free research and state power is entirely irresolvable by political means. Political power is obliged to apply the criterion of purpose in all its decisions. By contrast, the postulate of the basic sciences is that they are "free of purpose." It is in a certain sense a necessary pretense when someone explains to the public, with its expectations of purpose, that science sometimes involves asking basic questions from whose answers no results can be expected that would directly fulfill any purpose. I call this a lame pretense because, in truth, all research is basic research, and only through a secondary transformation can it address the problem of applying its findings.

One important point is that whoever exercises power and bears responsibility in the modern representative state needs to have this power and activity legitimized by ballot. This compels the politician to make only short-term calculations for four years at most. Science and research know no such short periods of time. There, the beginning, the first spark of a research idea, is separated perhaps by decades from anything that might be of use to society. We need only think of the upsurge of the natural sciences in the nineteenth century.

Up until the middle of this century it could justly be said that the preceding fifty years lived on the great research achievements of the nineteenth century, that it was the realization of the really productive ideas of the late nineteenth century that finally made the wave of industrialization foam and surge in the twentieth. Only with the atomic age, the splitting of the atom and the energy problems connected with it, has there emerged something really new in the application of research. In general there is a conflict between the short-term and the long-term, and its consequence is necessarily impatience on the part of the public sphere.

A further conflict that follows directly from this situation is the necessity of planning research and the near impossibility of doing so. For it really seems too much to ask that a researcher fulfill administrative expectations about the legitimacy and reliability of his plan. The researcher who impresses me is not the one who fulfills his plans but the one who finds something different from what he expected. On the other hand, from the planning perspective it is natural to demand too much of researchers because in economic, political, and every kind of practical planning the state depends on a certain reliability in its planning and the fulfillment of its plans, in order to establish its budget and its finances and distribute public funds justly.[2] The way society and its political forces set about organizing our social lives is at best a badly functioning accommodation that is full of compromise. But research allows no compromise.

It follows that it is almost impossible to control it. This needs to be said with a certain emphasis.

What is today required of the public sector in balancing the need and duty to oversee those who receive its money is complete nonsense when it comes to the research sector. The attempt to calculate how many hours a professor should spend in preparing his lectures and therefore how many hours in the week he is on duty so that public money can be paid out commensurately to him — the absurdity is palpable. It is not possible to administer research in this bureaucratic way. That financial oversight is necessary over the ever greater sums being invested in many branches of research certainly does have something convincing about it. But it must be admitted that this oversight is only partial. For who can really be in a position to judge whether the book purchases made by a particular library or faculty on December 15 of a certain year were as necessary as the specialists assert? Only those specialists themselves can make that judgment.

The purchases of the *Graeculi* are moderate, but in the natural sciences and medicine we are talking about much higher sums, and in the end it always remains the case — this is not a pathetic thing to say, but a simple description of the fact — that trusting the trustworthy is more effective than any financial control, which, like every other kind of control, always stays de facto within determinate limits. There is no doubt that trust can be abused. Wherever people show trust, the abuse of trust also occurs. But wherever trust is shown, that trust is also rewarded. There is a reason for trust between science and society. I believe there is common anthropological ground beneath the antagonisms between pragmatism and idealism and between practice and theory. But we shall certainly not find this ground if we agree to any false reconciliations.

It is a mistake to proclaim the virtues of making our practical political reason scientific, as people sometimes do these days. It is a mistake to make politics too academic, not least because the social sciences are still in their infancy compared to the natural sciences and do not have at their disposal a rich store of centuries of experience, but also because they lack the kind of comparatively patient object (in the sense of amenable to experiment and measurement) that has enabled progress to be made in the natural sciences.

It seems that one of the causes of our present difficulties is that we have forgotten about our power of judgment.[3] By "power of judgment," I mean what is called sound understanding, which generalizes from the experience of life. So those who exercise it in their political and social judgment do not use what has come to them through rules, books, or so-called teaching, but through experience (*Erfahrung*).[4]

Let us consider the anthropological foundations of the relation between theory and practice in human life. Is this relation really based on two irreconcilably different attitudes to human reason? Are the passion for theory and the passion for practice not simultaneously at work on both sides—on those who make a profession of theory and those whose profession is the practice of social life? Practice is not the blind application of theoretical findings about what it is possible for us to do. Practice, and politically responsible practice in particular, is imposed on man because he is not bound by the animal's natural instincts but is endowed with characteristics that have diverted us from the contexts and paths of pure naturalness. He is constantly faced with a choice. He sets himself ends and looks for means. He uses practical reason. He is familiar with organized work, which always involves the denial of impulses. Hegel was right when he said that work is desire held in check.[5] The immediate satisfaction of impulses is postponed in favor of a commitment of energy that is recognized as necessary, which also involves a commitment to social and legal order. This order is inevitable because in this sense man rationally shapes the conditions of his own life.

But this already leads to conflict, for none of it is possible without people having power over people. This is the problem of politics. The organization of a state is unthinkable without people exercising power over people, and what is so monstrous about it, the true dialectic of power, is that every attempt to control power gives birth to more power, even though the highly developed modern art of finding a balance of powers — as in, say, Montesquieu's doctrine of the separation of legislative and executive[6] — does to some extent bring about a certain equilibrium and control of power. This is the basic idea of the modern constitutional state. But we cannot forget that each controlling power is itself a possible new super-power within the constitutional order. This is part of the law of power itself.

Now, I believe that theory, the theoretical attitude, is likewise a fundamental form of human behavior, and that it is in no way limited to the special case that asks to be exempted from social expectations, that of science and research. For what is theory?

In the first place, theory involves and is, in my opinion, distance from oneself. In his great utopia, Plato showed that the guardians, the people who exercise control over power and thus hold the real power, can resist the law of constantly extending and overweening power only if there is something else that they would rather be doing.[7] This is the Greeks' idea of the theoretical life, which I do not consider at all out of date and which has merely been expelled from our conscious reflection by a certain over-emphasis on practice.

Theory is a basic human possibility, and it is connected most closely with those other organizations of power over men that we call the state, politics and pragmatic political action. What I mean is what Aristotle has already expressed with complete purity and truth: all men by nature strive after knowledge.[8] The curiosity of a child growing up, the first attempts at criticism, accumulating experience, the growing sense of direction, man's slow process of settling into the organized world that surrounds him, his participation in the linguistic communication of all with all—this all leads down the path of Bildung (cultivation). So cultivation is not the privilege of a particular class, and it is not a privilege that goes with any specially distinguished talents: Bildung is, as Hegel said,[9] the ability also to think from the other person's point of view. What characterizes the cultivated person is that he knows something about the particularity of his own experiences and so realizes the danger in generalizing which follows from that particularity.

My thesis: theory is just as primordial an anthropological datum as is practical and political power. So everything depends on constantly renewing the balance between these two human forces. And I am convinced that human society exists only because and as long as there is a balance of this kind.

The passion for politics involves an obsession with ends, the passion for theory involves a freedom from ends. This freedom from ends is virtually institutionalized in the sciences: they are *artes liberales,* not *artes mechanicae.* These free arts can also be called *schöne Künste,* fine arts, for "schön" (beautiful) has a much broader meaning than we might suppose from aesthetic taste.

The balance between obsession with ends and freedom from ends pertains to human life as such, however. It is human only if in our purposive action there is at the same time freedom from purpose. Whoever is able to achieve distance from himself, who gains insight into the limitedness of his sphere of life, and so openness to others, experiences constant correction by reality. Science has made this its most noble duty. Its freedom from ends serves to liberate us from those overly narrow ends that our wishes and illusions constantly create in us. This is the famous education to objectivity that makes a researcher.

A researcher's conscience consists in yielding unconditionally to the answer reality gives him, even if it means giving up years that he has invested in his research, only to find it leads to a blind alley. Education to objectivity and science, moreover, is a goal that can be accepted by society, and this implies that education to purpose-free research into truth is really not as odd as all that. It has nothing to do with the idolization of knowledge and ability. It is an indispensable element of the process of human "socialization" in which the practitioner, and even the "administrator," participate just as much as the researcher.

Inevitably, conflicts between the researcher and the administration keep arising. The institutionalization of free research, a sine qua non because it needs the millions upon millions invested in it, ultimately means that whoever allocates this money must answer for it, and so must justify its applicability. This demand can scarcely be realized without insoluble conflicts, bitterness, and exaggeration arising on both sides, with misconceptions all along the line. How is it possible to avoid bureaucratization and the dominance of a bureaucratic apparatus, so as to be critical of the particularity even of one's own administrative and political competence? For this there is no better way than the one Plato lays down for his guardian who would rather be doing something else than the task to which he is appointed. Someone who finds nothing more beautiful than power—and power must seem attractive if it is to be used effectively—will surely not be able to find that distance from himself and his power that would make a liberal use of his power possible. Liberalization of the way we treat scientific institutions and their possibilities seems to be bound up with the growing realization that what is beautiful, what is free from ends, is a self-fulfillment of humanity that is legitimate and needs no justification, and so is not a question of administrative techniques. Wherever administration functions, this insight will exist. But the public consciousness should really be informed of what, from its point of view, this really comes down to.

The problem that gives us so many headaches in rationalized

industrial society is, at bottom, a very old one. Modern scientific activity can lead to the same misreadings and the same corrections of these misreadings as was already the case for the creators of Western scientific culture, the Greeks. Thales of Miletus (624–544 B.C.), the founder of ancient philosophy, told the story of how he fell into a well on his way home and a maid had to help him out of it.[10] This anecdote was collected in a time when people thought the same thing about pure scholars as in many circles is still the case today. The point of the story is that Thales had climbed into the well to observe the stars, for the well was an ancient "telescope." That is how easy it is to be deceived about what a researcher is doing out of a passion for theory.

6

Science as an Instrument of Enlightenment

In his treatise on the question "What is Enlightenment?" Immanuel Kant gives his famous answer: "Sapere aude—have the courage to make use of your *own* understanding."[1] It seems a simple slogan—and yet it suggests something that unmistakably characterizes the spirit of modernity. For why should it require courage? What danger is threatening here? Now, making mistakes is certainly a universal danger for the human mind, and this is related to the fact that standing alone in one's opinion is oppressive—so much so that a person can come to feel as if he has been ostracized from the common faith, whereas on the other hand what he himself holds true seems so evident to him that he may clamor for it to be generally recognized.

It is in the critique of religion that we can see the real significance of defining the essence of enlightenment as having the courage to think differently in the face of all the dominant prejudices. In historical retrospect, we tend to describe the times when religion is criticized as times of enlightenment, and we distinguish a first and a second Enlightenment. The first Enlightenment took place in Greece, when the view of life enshrined in the epics and myths of Homer and Hesiod was dissolved by the new passion for discovery. In this sense the entire history of Greek thought stretching from Pythagoras to Hellenistic science is an age of enlightenment. Similarly, one can

A paper presented at the conclusion of a symposium on the history of science in Wolfenbüttel, 29 April 1972.

think of the modern Enlightenment as including the whole, long development that began with the Copernican revolution in astronomy, as a result of which the biblical view of life based on the story of creation had to be given up. Kepler, one of the great followers of Copernicus, had a slogan that expresses the moral force of this Enlightenment: "One has to have an open mind to be able to recognize the truth." It is a slogan that remained valid for Newton's time, and even for the spirit of present-day research.

Clearly both of these enlightenments have an especially close connection with science. But what was science for the Greeks, and what is it for modernity? Even the word the Greeks used for it, *mathemata*, indicates the paradigmatic role of mathematics. Plato stuck to this model so radically that he even saw the true science of the heavens, true astronomy, as consisting not in observing the actual positions and movements of the stars, but in pure mathematical and numerical relationships. And if in the end even nature came to be thought of as approximating these pure relationships of numbers and measurements, and if this approximation bestowed the character of science on, for example, medicine, it was still always compulsory assumptions and their consequences, the logic of proof, apodeixis (which is most purely embodied in mathematics), that constituted science.

On the other hand, though modern science is certainly also familiar with the dominance of the instrumentarium of mathematics, what distinguishes it from the sciences of pure reason — including philosophy, metaphysics, and above all mathematics — is that modern sciences understand themselves as sciences of experience. The logic of their procedure is called induction. A concept like "science of experience" would have sounded like "wooden iron" to Greek ears. Science requires no further experience. Yet in one respect the science that the Greeks established and that has determined all occidental culture is intimately allied with that of modernity: science exists and is important for no other reason than because it is "beautiful." But the beautiful is such that it is pleasing of itself and permits no disputing about why it is beautiful and pleasing. Thus broadly conceived, the beautiful (*kalon* in Greek) pertains to all theoretical science. It is the joy of theory, the joy of discovering the truth, that science lays claim to.

Certainly there is also a narrower sense of "Enlightenment"; this has been used to conceptualize a historical period, the eighteenth century, and was used so even then. The Enlightenment is tied to the critique of religion, and if it goes under the banner of science, then that implies the pragmatic relationship of science to human happiness, health, welfare, and freedom from suffering and misery. It promises a different kind of help from the consolation offered by the church. The feeling of the modern Enlightenment also corresponds to something in the first age of Enlightenment. The art of speaking and argumentation was disseminated as a universal means of achieving political and practical success, and so it is no accident that leaders of Greek sophistic, such as Protagoras and Gorgias, with their pragmatic relativism, encouraged skepticism and doubt about all science. Here a distinction between the first and the second Enlightenment appears with respect to the narrower concept of Enlightenment as well. The modern one appeals wholly to science, whereas in the end the ancient one finally turned against science.

This distinction is also manifested in their different attitudes toward religion. The first, Greek, Enlightenment differed so much from the modern one that metaphysics, as part and parcel of the development of Greek science, was to result from it in the form of rational theology (a metaphysics that remained valid for two thousand years). Ultimately, this first Enlightenment paved the way for acceptance of a new religion, the world religion of Christianity. In the modern Enlightenment the role of science has been quite different, which leads us to ask what science does signify for the modern Enlightenment. In asking this, I am thinking of the Enlightenments of both the eighteenth century and the twentieth. This is no misprint—it is a quite deliberate juxtaposition. Certainly if we speak of the Enlightenments of the eighteenth and the twentieth centuries, these are not two mutually independent developments. Science acknowledges only a constant progress. Yet we are entitled to speak of the Enlightenment of the twentieth century as something new. It was a tremendous upheaval, and it first achieved intellectual self-consciousness with the rise of Romanticism. Yet, however dizzyingly high were the expectations raised by the eighteenth-century Enlightenment's faith in reason, the French Revolution's great achievement, the emancipation of the third estate, signified less of a triumph of the Enlightenment than its spokesmen thought it did. It was, all in all, the beginning of the re-Christianizing of Europe. Who would have thought it possible at the end of the eighteenth century that a Vatican council would receive the church's unanimous approval of the edict proclaiming the pope's infallibility? Thus in many respects the nineteenth century was to become something very different from what might have been expected from the ideals of the Enlightenment. Instead of the equality of all, a real class society now came to be formed, in that "society" was distinguished from the proletariat. The countries of Europe developed into national democracies, some faster than others, despite the universality of the faith in reason. *Volkswirtschaft*, national economy, is a word that bears witness to the development that ultimately erupted so explosively in the period of the world wars.

And what of today? The episode is at an end. We are now

living in an age that is eliminating the retarding influences of the nineteenth century and laying aside all its taboos. All natural relationships have been fundamentally altered by the technical age's faith in science. Science governs through the society of experts. It is behind the global industrialization brought about by the world economy, it is behind the "electronic war," and Christianity has come to an end now that its secularized forms have suppressed the nihilism whose rise Nietzsche so clear-sightedly prophesied.[2] But this third Enlightenment's faith in science is dogged by nagging doubts about the future of mankind. This can and must give rise to reflection about the history of science. And so we ask how the second and the third Enlightenments have distinctive relationships to science. This way of asking the question is obviously rooted in the soil of the Enlightenment and takes the point of view of science in inquiring about the differences between the two epochs. But differences presuppose limits and so we must ask at the same time about the limits that have shaped the enlightenment impulse in each epoch.

Here we will be little concerned with the eighteenth century, known as the classical century of Enlightenment. It is certainly true that in that century the Enlightenment first became a public force; in the eighteenth century, too, the organized forms of science that institutionalized the public awareness of science first displaced the great pioneers of the sixteenth and seventeenth centuries who, as individuals, cleared the way for the new science. And it is true that the Enlightenment thereby first became a social factor.

Yet the epoch-making decisions had already taken place. When and how did modernity begin? With the Renaissance? That is, with humanism's re-awakening of antiquity? With the discovery of the individual (Jacob Burckhardt),[3] with the discovery of America? Whenever it started, it was certainly the new science that, for all its connections with ancient science, became something quite new and ushered in the new epoch. One can evaluate the various factors that led to this historical novelty very differently, and it remains an essential insight that if the concept of science changed fundamentally during this period, then this also had a theological basis. It is right to speak of the nominalistic background of the new science and of the way its theological grounding in the re-evaluation of, and over-emphasis on, God's omnipotence overshadowed both of the other classical predicates of God, his omniscience and his all-lovingness. The incomprehensible will of God prevents human reason from trying to penetrate God's thoughts. It has to be content with what is accessible to its own observations and its own relative knowledge and means of measurement.

Thus the new science brings with it the break-up of the linguistic view of the world in which the tradition used to live, for it applied the new language of mathematics to observation. So it was not new observations or progress in experience of the world, but rather a new projection of what it means to know that impelled the new science. Galileo, the creator of classical mechanics, had the clearest awareness of this, and it was actually not a sharpening of his observations but an imaginative wager that led him to discover the mathematically formulable axioms of mechanics. He was aware of this himself, and clothed it in the formula "mente concipio," not allowing himself to be discouraged by the fact that the law of falling he discovered did not correspond to any observable instances of falling, because emptiness, a vacuum, had not yet been produced anywhere. Galileo's founding of mechanics altogether excluded final causes from research into nature. He explained the processes of nature in terms of causal factors and their interplay, and this step enabled a new domination of natural processes. We call this domination "technology." But this technology is not a mere secondary consequence of the new knowledge of nature, or only of its technical presuppositions—it just transfers this knowledge into the practical realm, allowing us to calculate how we should intervene into initial conditions by making their effects calculable.

A new claim about what makes science science was here realized in an exemplary way. Descartes found the decisive new conceptualization for it. He gave the concept of method a new, dominant position. Method is, to be sure, an ancient Greek concept, and the Greek concept of method also meant approaching the thing to be known in a way appropriate to it. But the Greek concept of method took the criterion of its appropriateness from the individual character of the subject under consideration in each case. It was in opposition to this that Descartes developed the idea of a standard method—the idea of a universal method of verification, and so of avoiding error, which was supposed to succeed as long as the formal conditions of methodical procedure were met.[4] It is indicative of the tension between the new science and both the traditional form of knowledge and our practical orientation within the world that modern thought saw its task as thoughtfully integrating the two modes of knowledge. Descartes did not publish his *Discourse on Method* as an independent project of the new methodical thinking, but rather sought a compromise with the metaphysical tradition. The title of his most famous work displays this attempt at compromise: *Meditationes de prima philosophia*—that is, on metaphysics.

It is certainly characteristic of the modern Enlightenment at its outset that Descartes should have discovered the sure foundation of self-consciousness—whose apodictic certainty he took to be the paradigm of all evident knowledge—by way of doubting everything.[5] But it is no less characteristic of its beginning that this self-consciousness acquires legitimacy only from a roundabout appeal to the awareness of God that it itself contains. Thus this new and hard-won beginning was at the same time the beginning of the irresolvable confusion of modern thinking. It opened up three aporias. The first is the aporia of two substances. Extension and self-consciousness do not seem to belong to the same order of being at all. The second aporia follows from the first: the unsolvable problem of living things. The concept of extended bodies is insufficient for thinking about things that are actually alive. But the concept of self-conscious mind is also not applicable to living things that do not possess self-consciousness, so Descartes takes animals to be rather pitiful machines.[6] It was Kant who first integrated the two perspectives on living things by providing a philosophical grounding for and justification of the tension between the physical-causal and the morphological-final sciences of life.[7] His "solution" has governed our knowledge about living things ever since.

The third and most difficult aporia, whose resolution in the eighteenth century can once again be accredited to Kant[8] but which fatefully came to a head once more in the twentieth century, is the aporia of practical philosophy. The new concept of science is that of research. But research, as a never-ending empirical science, as an infinite process, must come into conflict with the present moment's practical need to know. In his so-called provisional ethics, Descartes himself had excluded ethics from the new science's claim to universality.[9] This new science neither can be nor wants to be the complete whole of knowledge in the sense that the older tradition was, and so how can it serve the need for practical certainty of life and the practical knowledge of action? A science understood as research must necessarily leave practical reason in the lurch.

Kant's response to this aporia rests on our sublime self-certainty about our moral freedom. Certainly we cannot understand theoretically how freedom is really possible because the whole of nature can be conceived only as a mesh of causal relations. But Kant saw that our practical reason requires that we act in self-consciousness of our freedom, that is, with an awareness of our responsibility, even if no theoretical solution to the aporia is possible. Kant's formula for the Enlightenment, "have the courage to make use of your own understanding," applies just as much to practical reason as it does to theoretical reason. For practical reason is not technical reason. It cannot submit to any received rules of behavior but must acknowledge what is unconditionally demanded, and cannot rest satisfied with what is expedient under particular circumstances.

If we view the ever-widening movement of Enlightenment in the second half of our century against this backdrop, what seems to be new is that technical thinking is beginning to expand into a universal view of the world. As the moral and religious basis of Kant's idea of freedom has vanished by degrees from present-day consciousness, man's self-consciousness has come to rest ever more exclusively on his ability to do and to make things. Our self-consciousness projects itself toward the technological dream and the emancipatory utopia.[10] So we can ask Kant's question anew—what does "enlightenment" mean or what could it bring about in this situation? Here we recall another Kantian description of the Enlightenment: it is mankind's outgrowing an immaturity for which it was itself to blame. In what way is mankind shamefully immature today, and what do we still need to enlighten ourselves about? It is hardly as though there were still blind faith in authority or an over-dominant priesthood in modern industrial society. I think it is our prepossession with the technological dream and our obsession with emancipatory utopia that represent the prejudices of our time and from which reflection, as the courage to think, needs to free us.

The technological dream bedazzles us when "can do" becomes "must do." The emancipatory utopia, for its part, is beginning to look more and more like the trauma of a freedomless world-bureaucracy. Historical reflection can lay bare the presuppositions that lie behind these prejudices. And it is reflection on the history of science that can enlighten us here. Both presuppositions, that of a perfect ability to make and that of a perfect ability to administer, correspond to the model of mechanics. The new tool of all tools—to recall Aristotle's famous remark that the hand is the tool of all tools [11]—is machine technology. This is the extended arm of man who, with the help of machines, can broaden his sphere of influence boundlessly. The historical scientific model of mechanics, always capable of calculating new effects and so bringing about new alterations, corresponds to a world of unlimited possibilities.

Today once again science promises enlightenment. For science tells us with increasing clarity that the world we live in is a world of limited possibilities. Our world is at an end if it keeps going on in this way, as if it were always about to "move forward." Science tells us that if we continue as we are doing, this end will befall us just as surely, even though the precise time cannot yet be exactly calculated, as if it had been predicted that the earth were going to collide with a star. This is especially what we learn from modern biology and everything known today as the problem of ecology. The population growth that seems to elude all control, the problems of food and water, environmental pollution, and especially the problem of energy all leave us in no doubt that the model of mechanics, with its endlessly outstretched arm, is founded on illusions. Today we have another scientific model that is more appropriate to the actual situation of humanity, the biological model of a self-regulated organism. This is the principle of regulatory feedback, which modern cybernetics has begun to clarify for us. To think of cybernetics as just another extension of the arm of humanity, enlarging still further our ability to make things, amounts, I think, to retaining an outdated and fatal form of thought. In fact, cybernetics offers more than a new technological possibility for further automation—it is a new world-schema, and the insights it brings present mankind with the task of engaging in critical self-reflection about our ability to make things. The question is not what can possibly be made but what can be made in such a way that it does not in the process destroy things that would otherwise be able to maintain themselves. The fundamental equilibrium of things must govern our thinking if we are to burn out the hydra of machines that constantly make new machines both necessary and possible.

It certainly seems paradoxical to want to make something that can maintain itself. That seems precisely to rule out all human efforts at creation. But we do possess an age-old example of this paradox: in medicine. Medicine does not produce anything, but it is always a restoration of equilibrium, its knowledge often surprised by new experience and its ability often outstripped by nature.[12] What can this example of constructive activity teach us? How can it contribute to our scientific understanding of the human situation today? What needs to be restored if we want to survive? Well, surely nothing but the consciousness of our real situation in the world. What we really have to do is alter our consciousness. The world must be known as something other than just as a world of unlimited possibilities. Science and the knowledge it provides encourage man more than ever before to think of himself as a steward of the earth, as someone who has to look after the place where he lives and works. This is the message modern science sends us, and it loses no credibility or urgency by the fact that it concurs with the religious message of creation theology.

The restoration of this kind of consciousness certainly seems to take us down a long and far-stretching path. So in the end we might consider doubting whether we can go down this path at all. I can see three objections that confront us: awareness of our predicament turns up first of all in the countries whose escalating industrial development forewarns us about the consequences of the path we are on. For countries with underdeveloped industry and civilization, however, this doubt about technological perfectibility fails to carry much weight, even if it manages to enlighten the social conscience of the industrial states and suggest political solutions. But what is involved here is a problem of humanity as a whole. That is so obvious that it makes an appeal to the consciousness of all as a common consciousness.

The second question, though, is whether time is not against us, in other words, whether it is not too late or would take too long to cultivate this collective consciousness. Here, however, it is important not to abandon ourselves to the illusions based on technical calculations about what it is possible for us to do that now threaten to turn negative: isn't it finally too late? Is the human race itself going to ruin? But who wants to be able to know or to calculate that? Again I think that medicine is a truer model. Doctor and patient here stand for humanity itself, and their two virtues of hope and patience are not false confidence and idle acceptance—on the contrary, they both allow for rational activity.

The third and perhaps the most serious objection lies in a human consciousness enamored of its ability to make things. Technological civilization puts a premium on the peculiar virtues of flexibility, adaptation, and fitting-in. The ideal of managing the world through technology still forms man in its image and makes him into a technical administrator who adequately fulfills his prescribed function without worrying about other people. This more than anywhere else, I think, is the bottleneck in our civilization, and this, more than anything else, calls for enlightenment. But enlightenment is still what it always was: it depends on judgment, on thinking for oneself and on cultivating these powers. So the present-day sense of the Kantian slogan of the Enlightenment, "Sapere aude—have the courage to make use of your own understanding," can be stated in a new way as the appeal to our social reason to awake from its technological dream.

7

The Idea of Tolerance 1782–1982

In 1782, Kaiser Joseph II issued the so-called "Toleranzpatent," a keystone in the eighteenth-century Enlightenment. Consider the significance of this event. It is the late eighteenth century. The Enlightenment has achieved conclusive victory. Even the rulers of this time, which we call the age of absolutism, are increasingly becoming enlightened despots.

The first representative of the Enlightenment on a European throne was the much-admired Friedrich II of Prussia. Other young monarchs, such as Catherine the Great in particular and also Joseph II and his successor Leopold II, followed Friedrich's widely admired example. In reading Goethe we see that even the son of a free imperial city who was never in the service of Prussia admired the Prussian king from his youth onward. It made a huge sensation when, in 1782, the Enlightenment movement broke through even into Catholic Austria and the capital city of the Holy Roman Empire of the German nation. We possess a small fragment of prose—"Der Hausball"—that Goethe presented to the Weimar court in the year 1783, portraying, in the style of a genre piece, the customs and morals of Vienna. It begins with an almost hymn-like portrayal of the anticipation with which the Vienna of that time welcomed the sunrise of Joseph II's reign from the foggy seas of the past.[1] The edict of tolerance publicly proclaimed the fruit that had

A paper given at the International Conference on Tolerance, Vienna, 15 March 1982.

ripened out of the Catholic Enlightenment and had slowly and irresistibly spread into the Habsburg countries.

What was this "Enlightenment?" We are faced with a number of different aspects of this phenomenon of the European Enlightenment. In particular, we must distinguish between the religious and the socio-political aspects of this movement. What gives this particular Enlightenment movement its edge and distinguishes it, for example, from the enlightenment that had led to the development of science in ancient Greece, is, first and foremost, that it is intimately concerned with the problem of religion, and of Christianity in particular. Natural reason must all along have found itself challenged in the extreme by Christianity's claims of revelation. God's becoming man and the mystery of the Trinity exceed its grasp; no rational theology can want to incorporate the things that the gospel reserves to faith. The development of modern natural science greatly aggravates this tension. I remember that when I was a child my father, who was a renowned natural scientist, simply could not brook the doctrine of the transubstantiation,[2] even though he was otherwise tolerant. It went against his scientific conscience. The same was always the case with the critique of miracles. The new methodical and scientific self-consciousness was able to accommodate this side of the biblical tradition to an extent only by complicated cultural-historical or psychological explanations, as the example of Spinoza shows.[3] On the other hand the church claimed to offer an absolutely exclusive path to salvation. The Christian command to missionarize was fundamentally absolute in that it branded those belonging to other religious confessions as infidels. Within European history this refers especially to the life and death struggle that the Christian West carried on against Islam, to which the city of Vienna bears glorious witness. Correlatively, on the other side, the Jewish community was ghettoized. As representative of the self-understanding of European statecraft, the Church exercised enormous influence, even after the Reformation—in the very name of the Counter-Reformation—against both Islam and Judaism, despite the schism of Christianity into two forms of faith. We can get some conception of this by thinking of Gotthold Lessing's *Nathan the Wise*. We recall how long he hesitated in finishing his favorite work and publishing it, his conviction (which turned out to be right) that it would create a powerful disruption, and the actual reaction that the work provoked.[4] *Nathan the Wise* appeared in 1779 and drove its author into a frightful new isolation. To be sure, it was first performed in Friedrich's liberal Berlin in the year 1783, but even in the age of Josephinism a performance anywhere else, least of all Vienna, would have been unthinkable.

Beyond its involvement in the history of religion and of the church, the Enlightenment signified a social movement dedicated to the political emancipation of the bourgeoisie. With the development of modern economics and science, an old tradition of municipal freedoms came into play that limited the absolutist claim of the worldly authorities, the kings and princes. Recently, Hermann Lübbe has rightly pointed out that the self-consciousness of the bourgeoisie was firmly grounded in the concept of *industria,* that is, of the flow of trade and its creations such as the machine halls and offices.[5] Even if, in the age of absolutism, the bourgeoisie understood itself and its freedoms only in a thoroughly negative manner and rejected any claim to rule, the ideal of bourgeois freedom necessarily had to solidify into a political claim. Even in the setting of the modern territorial state, the bourgeoisie, with its value-producing labor, could not in the long run renounce its claim to share in the political exercise of government. This is called "the emancipation of the bourgeoisie," which brought the third estate to equality in the outbreak of the French Revolution and gave rise to the slogan "civil rights," or rather universal human rights. We might mention a few further pieces documenting the general consciousness.

This is much the situation with Friedrich von Schiller's tragedy *Don Carlos*, which, during the very years of the Josephinian Enlightenment, gave a new political and social significance to a traditional dynastic family drama:[6] the introduction of the Marquis of Posa into Schiller's fiction lent a new and captivatingly eloquent voice to the rising bourgeoisie, its flow of trade, and its political potential. In the young Schiller's poetic imagination even the Spanish king, who represents the quintessence of absolutism and is furthermore portrayed as being strictly ruled by the church, can breathe the new air of freedom and falter for a moment.

Or we might recall how Mozart took Sarastro's morally and rationally based holy bond and religiously transfigured it in *The Magic Flute:*[7] here a human emotion is expressed that, at least within the compass of a magical play, has left all ecclesiastical and worldly dominion behind it. Its equivalent in the realm of ideas is Kant's foundation of religion, which he expressly said was "within the limits of reason alone."[8] Kant's foundation of "practical reason," which he radically disconnected from all eudemonistic perspectives (even understood as the Christian promise), signified a milestone in the ideological emancipation of the bourgeoisie that preceded their political emancipation in the revolution. An interesting but not widely known fact might illustrate this matter further and especially throw some light on the history of influence[9] that the edict of tolerance has had: in the 1790s a four-volume translation of Kant's works into Latin appeared in the court of the Austrian monarchy, plainly produced for them; this is a symbol of the willingness and readiness of the Catholic Enlightenment to reconcile the new thinking with the sanctified tradition of metaphysics and the authority of the Christian church.

This defined the place that the edict of tolerance was to occupy 200 years ago. What defines the framework to which it belongs is the state Christian religion, which in the Habsburg countries was Catholicism, because of the principle "cuius regio eius religio."[10] The edict of tolerance is a political measure signifying a softening of hardened fronts with a view toward the toleration and liberation of divergent religious denominations. This religious tolerance evidently presupposes that the system of government and the Christianity of society go unchallenged. Tolerance is an expression of strength, not of weakness. It does not mean recognizing the equal rights of those who think differently. What is tolerated is confined to the sphere of private mental life and extends at most to the practice of an individual's own worship. If the enlightened King of Prussia had offered a formulation for his act of shrewd statesmanship, it might have run: "Here everyone can go to heaven after his own fashion." This was not exactly an expression of religious devotion, but of the strength of the state's new awareness that it could afford to relax its control. Today the state knows that it owes its executive power to religious tolerance and the civil right to freedom, and this stems from the unbroken heritage of the Enlightenment.

We can now describe the situation in 1982, by considering the broadening horizon within which our political and human consciousness must move. We must again start from the assumption that a new wave of enlightenment is raging, this time over more or less the whole of mankind: the scientific domination of nature and the transformation of our natural environment is changing the face of the earth and impelling us toward a rational construction of our social world. The world-wide universality of this enlightenment effects a massive change in criteria in two respects.

On the one side there is religion: it is now no longer limited to the sphere of the Christian tradition but has entered into a whole new field of tension. Not only does it now have to do with the world religions' dialogue with each other; they must all come to grips with atheism as well. For the first time in human history, forms of political organization have developed in which atheism represents the state religion in the same way that Christianity was the state religion of Europe for hundreds of years. What is extraordinary about this fact is that it relativizes the distinctions among the great world religions. Each of them must certainly continue to hold that its own doctrine and its own faith are the true doctrine and the true faith, and yet scientific atheism and its political organization represent a viewpoint from which—politically considered—all the differences among religions seem less serious. Certainly no religion can of itself be in a position actually to recognize the relative authority of other religions. Even within Christianity it is not easy to make progress toward ecumenical understanding between the denominations. On the other side, the alteration in world-wide criteria has meant that Christianity has necessarily lost its absolute standing in humanity's great conversation with itself. We do not know how other cultures whose religious traditions are different from ours will raise their voices in this conversation. The world's religions are necessarily discovering that they have something in common of which they had not hitherto been aware and which points far beyond anything that has come to light in previous attempts at dialogue. There has already been one epoch—that is, the eighteenth century— that was prepared to recognize Chinese wisdom as a particular contribution to the rational religion of mankind. Similarly in the nineteenth century, the Romantics attempted to discern in Indian wisdom a heightened and enriched form of Christian redemption. These were fruits of the modern Enlightenment. But we must admit that something like the mystery of the Trinity, which is central to the history of our own faith and thinking, seems quite inconceivable from, say, an Islamic point of view. Christianity's claims to be absolute, or for that matter the truth claims of any religion, no longer go uncontested. We ask ourselves whether the idea of tolerance formed within enlightened Christian countries is sufficient to stand against hardened ideological positions that have developed in the struggle to dominate the earth. What can tolerance mean when nobody, perhaps not even the religion of atheism, is so sure of his ground that he can rationally establish his own claim, in the way that the European Christian state society was sure of itself centuries ago?

And how does this look from a socio-political point of view? The emancipation of the bourgeoisie, which may be considered complete in the modern democracies, has led as it were to the self-dissolution of the bourgeoisie. Its counterpart, the classless society, proclaimed to be the creation of the workers and the peasants, has something abstract about it in comparison to the uniform appearance of today's industrial society, which has shaped the face of the advanced industrial nations and drawn their features everywhere, even if they often seem to be drawn only as a mask behind which there lurks an unknown face. This situation has given the concept of tolerance a new profile. Thus, I think it significant that the problem of religious tolerance now seems to be the last problem we should worry about rather than the first; it is an accurate reflection of the conditions within which we now operate that we should instead pay special attention to the role of economics. I ask myself: what can tolerance mean under such altered circumstances? What are we so certain of that we can or should practice tolerance—or do we have to say that anything whose life is not ruled by hard dollars exists at all thanks only to tolerance? Like culture, for example?

This inquiry brings us to the topic: tolerance and the problem of the generations. Everybody knows at once what we are talking about here. What is not quite so certain is who we are supposed to be urging to be tolerant in our reflections about the value of tolerance. The older generation? Parents? The changes pervading our social world have taken on such a breathtaking pace that the basic presupposition of all tolerance—namely, our being ruled by self-evident common convictions that shape our social life—is precisely what is really missing. Neither the older nor the younger generation, which is bewildered by its need for orientation, seems to fit the pattern within which the conflict of generations has always been played out. What has become today of the definitive authority of the older generation, which formerly could behave tolerantly or intolerantly toward its juniors, and how can the succeeding generation focus its drive toward emancipation when it finds that everything is allowed and everything is accessible? What drives young people to intolerance is not certainty about their new values but a mysterious lack of orientation.

The wave of industrialization and bureaucratization sweeping over us has dissolved once self-evidently binding traditions into untested arbitrariness. This happens in the name of the "freedom that I love." But what does this freedom look like? Let's take an example: the feeling of freedom that, especially for young people, comes from having their own car is coupled with an enormous dependency, and leads to both a leveling and an isolation unknown to travelers of earlier times. People do certainly gather together in front of the television screen, which deceptively poses as a freely available and ubiquitous source of information that is common to everybody. But in fact it signifies the end of conversation,[11] the extreme isolation of each individual, and therefore the enormous loss of freedom that results from our inevitable dependence on media politics. In the same way, the freedom of the new unconventionality that pervades our whole social life—especially that of the young—is coupled in a peculiar way with a feeling of helplessness and impotence. The source of this impotence is no longer other people, those who control and dominate us, but the "system."

This obviously refers to the immanent lawfulness of the economic and technical processes that are the real dominant figures of our day. It is largely independent of the various democratic and totalitarian political systems on which our states are organized. The ideologization of the political fronts cannot obscure this fact. Intolerance displays its weakness. One can certainly say that the "system" of modern industrial society and its universal dominion over the administered world has developed from the same motives that gave victory to the idea of religious and spiritual tolerance in the Enlightenment. But it is precisely the universality with which the Enlightenment has triumphed that endangers its own offspring, tolerance. There is something dictatorial about the ideal of scientific rationality (*Rationalität*) that it is imprudent to disobey. Typically, when this ideal is put into practice in social reality, it is known as "rationalization." How changed is the tone of this word, whose noble derivation from *ratio*, from reason, is plain for all to see! "Rationalization" suggests transforming the environment into a controllable organization based on a rational planning, rational methodicality, and rational efficiency that is all-embracing and total. To fail in this seems to be unpardonable negligence. We know from the totalitarian political systems of our time—as we do from similar ancient states (before the Christian church limited the state's omnipotence)—that no totalitarianism is conducive to tolerance.

This is what Schiller was talking about through the mouth of the Marquis of Posa, when he talked of furthering freedom of thought—the universal conformism that knows no considered decision but only accommodation to those in power and their supposed or actual opinions. What gives state power its total presence is not so much its external pressure as the inner reaction it produces. Pragmatism, conformism, and the rewarding of adaptability (as Schiller saw) become victorious over the cultivation of individual judgment and original imagination. That is the real "terror" that comes from power. Anyone who has survived the time of a regime of terror, as I have, knows that we ourselves helped give immediate terror a kind of omnipresence: the real power of the state secret police lay in anxiety about its unpredictability. It is really a myth that a state secret police knows everything. Its presence is probably always an extremely limited one. But there is something in this: domination that is based on force and not on consensus has to be feared, and is effective for exactly that reason. The less a government is based on consensus, the more it has to behave in a totalitarian way—and tolerance then necessarily appears to be weakness. When the people it governs experience its activity as purely arbitrary, it undermines its own possibility from within. Nobody can depend on it. It is the peculiar nature of tolerance that the field of play within which things are tolerated never has precise limits. Toleration means something quite different from law. Only where deeper solidarities are in play—for example, an enlightened state's interest in eliminating interdenominational discord—can tolerance be possible as a virtue.

It seems that what we find today is this: where rationality (Rationalität) represents the ultimate criterion, its claim to validity becomes "total." This unquestionably applies to the rationality that controls our economic system and the administration of the modern state. For just this reason the ideal of planning and administration that expects all government and domination to be abolished by radically rationalizing all living relationships has had such a great attraction for both political utopias (since Saint-Simon[12] or even since ancient sophistic) and utopian politics.

Now, it has to be said that the task of politics has always been to base the government of men on actual solidarity[13] and factual consensus. It may be that patriarchal forms of life inherently approximate this ideal. In any case, it is unrealistic for any form of state or government to postulate any kind of harmony between the people and the state, because every form of power, not just that of a tyrant or an absolute ruler, is dedicated to increasing its own power. The whole doctrine of politics and the constitution of states thus aims toward a consensus of the governed, and tries to restrict the extent to which those in power can attain further power. But this presupposes solidarity, which cannot be created by any constitution. Nietzsche drew the most radical consequence of this when he recognized the will to power as a universal principle and found it at work not only in the rulers but also precisely in the things that hold them back—for example, law courts, governing bodies, etc.— and even in those who serve them.[14] But then what can the solidarity that lets us all live together be founded on?

At the beginning of our century Max Weber, the great sociologist, was already predicting that the world would progressively lose its magic through growing bureaucratization.[15] Since then we have seen how inevitable this process is. It holds sway throughout our social system, literally from birth to death, and there is not a political system in the world that seems to know any remedy for it.

This should not at all be confused with the distinction between a single-party and a multi-party state. When the power of the state is ideologized and it claims to possess the one true doctrine, this leads with an inherent logic toward the elimination of anyone who thinks at all differently—as in the Inquisition—which might mean physically annihilating them or treating them as mentally ill. But almost more ominous, because it is imperceptible, is how the mass media influences our opinions and consequently weakens our judgment.[16] The idea of comradeship used by modern totalitarian systems cannot obscure the pressure to toe the party line. The sense of community that it reveals has all the exclusivity of intolerance. But can parliamentary democracy and the division of power, where the multiplicity of positions and interests find their balance, count as a system of public pluralism? If the consensus of all is no more than an anonymous election, then it is certainly significant that political opponents in parliament always refer to one another as "colleagues." This terminology from ancient Roman civil law lives on wherever the stress is placed not on opposition but on the solidarity that can unite and reconcile even the most entrenched opponents. But even in legislative bodies and within the scope of the decisions they make, bureaucratization and the automation of administration really run unchecked. We might think of the party machine that restricts the representative's freedom of choice, or of politicians' reliance on experts.

This condition is manifested in the concept of "function" and the role of the functionary. This term expresses how each person and every function is subordinated to a system and dependency on that system. Not just states and confederations of states, but all the various interest groups whose antagonism defines our political landscape, and even the economic systems that try, in countless variations, to balance the power, or rather the intervention, of the state and the free activity of workers and entrepreneurs, are all interwoven with one another in so many different ways that we can plausibly speak of a single system of world economics and a single problem of world administration and the prevention of war. Every area of our lives has been integrated into this system and is now administered by it alongside everything else. Its influence extends from so-called family life to the so-called culture industry. It seems inevitable: economics is our fate.

From the state of affairs I have outlined, it becomes clear what has been coming to fruition in individual minds, or even in the convictions of small circles of people, and has now led to an almost universal reaction among young people: uneasiness about culture. It also becomes clear that this can lead to emotional outbursts. Precisely because it has become a tangible certainty in this system that everything depends on everybody, the individual, indeed, whole generations of individuals see themselves as having been, as it were, robbed of their freedom—the freedom of initiative. The consequence of this is the purposeless call for adaptation; and if most people resign themselves to playing roles they do not enjoy in fulfilling whatever function happens to fall to them, it is not always the worst people who try to escape. Certainly anyone who questions the power-monopoly of the modern constitutional state testifies in doing so to his own helplessness. Such an individual becomes entangled in that contradiction long ago outlined by Plato's *Crito*:[17] wanting to exclude oneself from something one has already accepted.

We have all accepted the system under which we live. Max Weber already used to insist on this in his time,[18] in his opposition to Romantic ideology and the esotericism of the George circle. Absolute domination is no longer that of one individual or a dominant class, however, but of a system. There is no despot that could be driven from the throne, only an anonymous domination that governs all. Now this is where the idea of tolerance gains a new significance, precisely because tolerance can no longer be demanded of the one or the few who have power. In the end nobody has power and everybody is in service. But for just this reason, tolerance becomes a universal duty. In point of fact, the history of this idea shows how, through being invoked in constitutions and religious edicts, tolerance has expanded beyond its original political meaning into a universal moral requirement. Like all moral values, we become especially aware of it and put it into words when someone neglects or offends against it. Thus it is intolerance that we all want to avoid being reproached with. The high hymn to tolerance that Lessing's Nathan strikes up with the fable of the three rings[19] displays the continuity between religious toleration and the universal human virtue of tolerance. Thus religious truth ultimately proves to find its expression in human moral tolerance.

Herein lies something significant revealed by the above mentioned relation of strength, safety, and generosity to tolerance and conversely the proximity of intolerance to weakness: tolerance is not the hesitation that concedes the other's rights because it puts no trust in its own rights and power. The statesman may profess general tolerance in religious things out of indifference and skepticism, as perhaps in the case of the enlightened skeptic on the Prussian throne. But he too does this not out of weakness but out of the strength of his civic consciousness and trust that the power of this civic consciousness in his subjects holds the state together.

We can discern the connection of tolerance with strength and intolerance with weakness when, say, freedom of speech is limited by censorship. The degree of leniency in censorship corresponds to the level of the government's strength and security, and so also to the strength that can be attributed to public opinion and can be counted on. But we should not equate tolerance and freedom of speech just like that. In political life there are always limits to the freedom of speech and publication. In wartime, for example, these freedoms are most restricted, just because that is when the commanders are most endangered. And the impressive freedom of speech that characterizes, say, American society, and that can directly increase respect and admiration for divergent opinions and for the socially and politically excluded, should not be allowed to conceal the fact that it is precisely there that the pressure of social conventions can intensify into a witch-hunt, especially where certain explosive topics ("colored" people, anti-communism, sectarianism) come into play.

Similarly, in human social intercourse there is a degree of tolerance that expresses the strength or weakness of one's own position and one's own nature. For example, we generally consider someone intolerant if they cannot bear being contradicted, and yet for our own part we would not lay claim to being unconditionally and indiscriminately tolerant of others—when we are of another opinion, for example, we don't always give voice to our objection. Thus there is also something like self-censorship. However much candor and mutual trust people's relationships display, it is all embedded in that friendly, courteous, considerate, and appreciative style of intercourse that we notice when we consider how weak human self-confidence (everybody's self-confidence, we must presume) really is. In itself this is not so much tolerance as respect for the limits of the tolerance one can expect from others; but even this is still tolerance, and its neglect intolerance.

So tolerance is at work in all of this not only as a virtue of social intercourse that has been bred into us, but also as a basis for that human way of thinking that reckons on the otherness of the other and the multiplicity of othernesses that exist alongside one another in our complicated and diversely tangled reality. This one world in which we all live is marked by a diversity of languages, religions, cultures, and traditions that, in spite of the scientifically based rationality (Rationalität) that is valid for all of us, or in the end precisely because of it, represents a problem of tolerance that is hardly less severe than those of earlier times with the ruling orthodoxies of various churches and religious denominations. Certainly the religious and especially the denominational problem of orthodoxy has lost some of its currency in comparison with what it had, say, in the age of the counter-Reformation and the supremacy of the Inquisition, and likewise the civil constitutional state has disarmed the political problem of tolerance. On the other hand, we can see that new confrontations leading to intolerance are always arising from the way distances are being closed up by modern transportation, telecommunications technology, and all the other possible modern forms of mobility. We might think of the separatist tendencies in countries where language, religion, or economic factors endanger the unity of a state that has evolved in the course of history.

This makes all the clearer the moral duty of tolerance that is a duty for each and every human being. With the dwindling of collective ties and their self-evidence, it seems to have become a new absolute duty. When people are not bound by any other kind of community that might in some sense predetermine the breadth of tolerance they afford one another, and when, conversely, the clashing of interests among groups and their organizations demands to be adjudicated, the ideal of a legally secured order truly rules unchecked and so the tyranny of function becomes the only decisive social factor. The tyranny of function is the tyranny of the system into which we are incorporated and which compels us, as it were, to identify with it. We are aware of this from the degree of intolerance that our official duties impose on us. It takes no small measure of self-distancing to keep oneself free from the pressure of this identification, or to break free from it at the right moment. The thoroughgoing rationalization and functionalization of all areas of life do not so much promise a social constitution based on power-free consensus as revitalize all the aspects of intolerance that are intrinsic to the desire to govern and pursue one's interests. The intolerance of power that is worried about its power has, as it were, shattered into its integral elements and has then completely set in again. So in the end, we think just as we did 200 years ago when Habsburg Austria was professing religious tolerance. Tolerance has again become the rarest of all virtues, but today it cannot be proclaimed in an edict.

8

Isolation as a Symptom of
Self-Alienation

The job of philosophy is to clarify concepts, not to present a
new body of knowledge acquired through empirical research.
On the path toward the clarification of concepts, we need
an answer to the question "Is isolation a symptom of self-
alienation?" What is a symptom? It is that by which something
—an illness, for example—is recognized. Its logical structure is
to be something manifest in which something hidden and dangerous becomes visible. The ancient Greeks described their attitude toward research like this: the visibility of what is hidden
lies in what shows itself. Thus no causal connection is implied
in the concept of the symptom. It is not claimed that the symptom is the immediate effect of what it points to, but that there
must be some indirect connection between a symptom, which
makes something recognizable, and what is made recognizable
by it. So it is always appropriate to pose alongside the question
of whether isolation is a symptom of self-alienation the further
question whether self-alienation is a cause of isolation.

ISOLATION AND SOLITUDE

The first thing to notice is that we are talking here about isolation and not solitude. So the first question we must ask ourselves is whether there can ever be isolation for anyone who is
familiar with solitude. Isolation is a form of loss. What is lost
in it is nearness to others. In the experience of isolation there

A public lecture given in Bern, 4 July 1969.

seems to be suffering along with the solitude. But solitude is really a very ambivalent phenomenon. Not just philosophers, but anyone who really wants to think about the experience of solitude must deal with two very different aspects of it. Solitude is not always a suffering. To be sure, it presents itself that way at first. There is being forsaken by one's friends—one thinks of Job or Christ on the Mount of Olives.[1] To be forsaken by friends is to be deprived of the supporting nearness of others. Now, this being forsaken by the supporting nearness of others can be viewed as a very close neighbor of that other forsaking with which we are familiar—being forsaken by God. Even in talk of a "god-forsaken place" we can hear the original God-forsakenness of Christ's last words on the cross.[2] In any religious experience there is an inner connection between the forsakenness of the nearness of others and the forsakenness of God. It is not only Christ's commandment of love that sees love of one's neighbor and one's relationship with God together. There is also a lovely Greek phrase of Euripides: "To embrace friends, that is God."[3] What the Greeks wanted to bring to expression here is the same as what Hölderlin once called the social sphere that is God.[4] In this conceptual definition, the opposite of solitude is implied: to stand in a communal sphere and to be supported by something communal. The affliction of isolation inflicts on us the diminution and the loss of this communal support.

But being deserted by the support of communality is surely only one side of the phenomenon of solitude. Solitude can also be sought. If we want to pose the problem of man's self-alienation in society on the right plane of questioning at all, then we shall have to immerse ourselves in this phenomenon for a while. I suppose the quest for solitude is essentially a discovery that was brought into the general consciousness by Rousseau. In many German towns there is a *Philosophenweg*, a "philosophers' path:" there's an especially famous one in Heidelberg. For those with an ear for history, this "philosophers' path" is not named after the philosophy professors. We should rather understand a "philosopher" as someone who has a remarkable inclination for walking through the area alone. That is the original meaning of the common street name Philosophenweg. Indeed, it really isn't obvious that anyone would want to go for a walk alone. Perhaps that's just peculiar to the age of introspection, and to the search for the innocence of nature amid the corruption of morals—if I may, with Rousseau, express myself so critically of culture.

Now, what is sought in the quest for solitude is not actually solitude, but "abiding" with something, undisturbed by anyone or anything else. So what one is looking for on the philosophers' path is not really solitude at all, but the soft breathing of nature that takes one up into his life as if through a gesture of sympathy. Goethe has the harpist sing: "Who devotes himself to solitude, alas, is soon alone."[5] What this line means is that solitude can hold an attraction for the human soul, can even arouse an intoxication that wards off anything that might disturb the intimacy of this condition. The quest for solitude is always the desire to hold on to something.

Thus the *lover* seeks solitude because he is completely filled by yearning: this being-held-onto by something absent, which could not be replaced by any possible presence. Solitude also exists in an unsought way for the *elderly*. They obviously have the scent of solitude about them. Because an old man can and does look back on too much, he is beyond the reach of other people. One thinks of the marvelous pictures of solitude in Rembrandt's late period—the solitude of the eye that gazes toward us from the shadow: it sees nothing more because it expects nothing more, since it is no longer looking forward but back into itself. Another form of solitude that besets one unsought is the solitude that is concealed in *power*. The powerful man is solitary. It is the curse of power that the anticipated will of the powerful gets reflected back to him along the thousand paths of flattery: great powerful men have always also been great despisers of men. Flattery and fear weave the veil of solitude that surrounds the powerful. Again, we must not mistake the solitude of the *wise man* for forsakenness. His path is solitary because he does not share the interests of others; since he is so experienced and his view of reality so free of illusion, it is not possible for him to share in others' intoxication. The great example of such solitude is Zarathustra in Nietzsche's poetical fiction,[6] who has to seek solitude again and again. What makes him so solitary is his knowledge, a knowledge that divides him from all others and pursues him throughout the whole history of his solitary life: the insight into the breakdown of all existing values. Finally, *religion* tells us that solitude is to be sought: in Christianity, we are familiar with the solitude of prayer, which goes back to the solitude of the Son of Man.

Solitude, then, is something quite different from isolation. Isolation is an experience of loss and solitude is an experience of renunciation. Isolation is suffered—in solitude something is being sought.

Self-alienation and Social Compulsion

Our preliminary examination shows us that the familiar social phenomenon of self-alienation is close to isolation. The concept of self-alienation is an expression of a social sickness—perhaps also of suffering in society. Alienation always presupposes an original intimacy and is experienced as an increasing alienness. When two people become estranged from one another, each senses an alienation from the other person who was once close to him. That is still not a separation, not yet a breach, but a mounting uneasiness that the familiar closeness is becoming false. The intimacy has not yet vanished, but just seems to be dwindling. For someone who becomes isolated, this experience of dwindling intimacy becomes intense. The world of nearness becomes altogether more and more alien to him. A well-known part of isolation's tendency toward inner self-involvement is that a person can no longer extricate himself from it and approach other people, but seems instead to have drowned in it. So isolation does always have something to do with man's becoming a stranger in the world and in the human world as a whole.

But such isolation is still far from being the self-alienation of man in society. I should ask, therefore, what the intimacy is that becomes alien there. The answer can only be that work, as one's own work, becomes alien to man. That obviously implies that work essentially determines one's self. That is self-evident to us, but in truth it signifies that work—the only new god of our age—is the last worldly god of the polytheistic tradition still to be honored among us. What could lead to its seeming to be no longer our own work?

It is not only in modernity that human society is founded on the division of labor in which an individual's work satisfies not just his own immediate needs but common needs. And it is just as clear that in this system for satisfying common needs through divided labor the concept of a need is very loosely defined. It is debatable precisely what people's divided labor is supposed to provide: is it the necessities of life, or is it more than that? Is human society possible at all when work produces only the necessities? It is worth considering to what extent what the Greeks called *to kalon*, the beautiful in the broad sense of a free surplus and superfluity, is that whereby human society satisfies itself as human.

The form in which the division of labor is now organized, and determines the individual's place in society, is termed one's profession. A profession has the form of indirect identification with the universal. For "profession" patently means that the specific tasks and responsibilities arising from an individual's activities are consciously legitimated through the universal. We shall still have to ask ourselves what are the effects of having a profession for the life of society as a whole. To me, one thing seems certain: that the decreasing possibility of identifying with the universal is what we call the self-alienation of man in society.

The complaint about the self-alienation of man was already making itself heard in the age of the Enlightenment. Friedrich von Schiller's letters "On the Aesthetic Education of Man"[7] speak of the dead, soulless machine-state in which each individual works only as a cog or a link without—to state the meaning of this metaphor—his individual consciousness being connected with the activity of the whole. It is against the dead soulless machine-state that Schiller, in his magnificent letters, sets up the idea of the free activity of man and a state of freedom, and proposes the remarkable Weimar excursus on play and the state of aesthetic education. It was Schiller's impulse that led Karl Marx—who put the self-alienation of man down to the artificial relations of production, the fetishization of money, and the commodification of human labor—directly to his critique of the capitalist economic system.[8]

These things are well known. The self-alienation of man then applied to a particular class situation, and designated the employers' exploitation of the proletariat. When we reconsider the phenomenon of self-alienation, the problem arises under greatly altered circumstances. Today the self-alienation of man in society can no longer be spoken of as the domination of one class by another class that alone enjoys freedom—as in the case of the consciousness of the master who uses the servile consciousness and lives off the work of the servant. We live in a modern social welfare state. What we experience there is that we all lack freedom, and that seems to me to be the self-alienation that concerns us today.

What is it based on? What is this lack of freedom that everybody experiences today? Everyone immediately thinks of the professional consciousness that I started out with, and which included a direct reference to the universal. Today, through the rationalization of the ways in which human work is deployed, this consciousness has suffered a curious limitation, so that the basic consciousness of man in our thoroughly rationalized society is really that each individual is replaceable. This, I think, is where the reasons are to be found why we are denied identification with the universal.

Let's describe a few forms of this denial. They are experiences of compulsion. But what strange kind of compulsion can this be, to which we are exposed only by our own experience? It is not the compulsion of a master, of somebody stronger, or of any superior who dictates our actions. If it were, we should always be able to fight against it with our own powers of resistance. What gives us the feeling that we lack freedom is rather our insight into the *rational obligation* (rationale Sachzwang) that dominates us all. The individual's initiative in trying to find a way that he can work for the universal is oddly paralyzed by the complexity of the social system of production and labor in which we live: we experience this again and again in all sorts of ways. Our thoroughly rationalized society suffers from something similar to what psychiatrists call the repetition compulsion. The repeating of actions compulsively seems to be a good simile for the essence of "administration." Administration wants us to do as we have done in the past. In order to be administered, our world has to be made uniform, and so it is not malice that rejects every innovation: we know in advance what has to be done, and how. Anyone who would like to do otherwise finds himself condemned by the rational obligation to take up a position that is not of itself transparent to him. This already explains why animosity toward our cultural world is becoming so noticeable, especially in the younger generation.

Or we could look at another experience of such compulsion, again one that is just as innocent as it is hard and tyrannical. I mean the compulsion to consume, something that hardly anybody can avoid who does not possess a great measure of inner freedom. For the organization of consumption and selling is virtually compelled by our whole economic system. It is not really possible to escape, in any kind of free determination of needs, from the consumer goods provided by industry and the economy, when the flood of uniformly generated consumer desires sweeps us, so to speak, in through the doors of the department stores.

Behind this there is a still deeper compulsion, which I consider the most serious of these compulsions. We are compelled to believe certain things: not because we are commanded to, but just because they come sugared with the sweet poison of information politics. We are all constantly exposed to a flood of information from which we cannot escape. A child that grows up without a television pays for it early—one look at that child's school essays shows that he doesn't know the rubrics under which this wave of information has channeled the universal consciousness. The consequence of this is belief-compulsion; for the information is no longer direct, carried from me to you in a conversation, but is always mediated by a selective agency—the press, the printed word, radio, and television.[9] In democratic states these agencies are in turn privately controlled, but we are still aware of the extent to which the obligation of keeping to the tried and tested ways of doing things restricts initiative and the possibility of actual control. In other words, compulsion is still occurring here. It seems that anyone who thinks that some person must be responsible for this has not completely woken up to the gravity of our situation. The self-alienation of man in modern society is a universal one, and it is coupled with the awareness of an unfathomable dependence and alienness, so that an individual's work not only seems meaningless to him, but contributes to a sense of general, unfathomable alienness. It is this lack of freedom that is experienced as the self-alienation of man in society.

It induces us to withdraw into our private shells. But whoever takes this path experiences at the same time the impossibility of withdrawing. For if I seek the "lamplight of the private" (as Marx called it), all I do is hide from myself the dependencies that determine me without my being able to detect them. Precisely in a liberal political system, we all have to pay for every lapse of political solidarity, because we can't hope to avoid our common fate just by ducking and hoping that the lightning will strike elsewhere.

Friendship — With Others and with Oneself

This experience of unfathomable dependencies now clarifies the contrary claim, which we can designate as a completely social consciousness. The communality that is missing from our lives is extrapolated into the form of a consciousness that takes up the cause of the future of society as its very own affair. This kind of consciousness manifests itself today in the accusation that our parents' generation is responsible for the universal lack of freedom that I have described. It manifests itself just as much in our being satiated with prosperous civilization as it does in the flight toward utopias. It also manifests itself in the way that every restriction is experienced as an injudicious repression. There's a new word that is symptomatic of this; I heard it recently when an interviewer on the street was asking people "Warum hört der Leidensdruck eigentlich nie auf?"

(Why does the pressure of suffering never really stop?) This new word "Leidensdruck" (pressure of suffering) seems to bespeak our warding off all experience of reality. For experience of reality is experience of challenges and opposition, and it is never without suffering, as well as the overcoming of opposition. Leidensdruck, on the other hand, sounds like something we escape by getting drunk, or by immersing ourselves in collective activity. Privacy is certainly not to be placed above all else, and it is worth being able to sacrifice our private interests to communal tasks. But there is something lacking in the fundamental conditions of human community if the demands of modern society are experienced as the pressure of suffering that is even more to be warded off than the suffering of isolation. Complaining about the pressure of suffering is just another way to deny one's isolation, and it bears witness to complete self-alienation: our society is entering further and further into this danger-zone. For it is part of the negative ideal of liberation from the pressure of suffering that no positive identification with the universal justifies the experience of challenges and restrictions.

It is worth going back to the most ancient insights here. One of the greatest lessons we can learn from the Greek classics is the central significance accorded to friendship in Greek ethics. In modern ethical works, the most coverage the problem of friendship ever gets is a thin chapter in some appendix. In Kant we find the beautiful and thought-provoking expression: "a true friend must be as rare as a black swan."[10] But that's about all he has to say on the subject. In Aristotle's Ethics, on the other hand, it occupies the central main section and makes up a quarter of the whole.[11]

What is friendship? The Greek word for it is *philia*. This concept comprehends so many dimensions! It includes every form in which men live together, and refers to business relations and teamwork as much as to camaraderie in war or married life, and the formation of social groups and political parties — in short to the entire life of the human community. What is still called *Parteifreundschaft* in German today is a last echo of this ancient Greek generic term. As an old Pythagorean saying has it, part of the essence of friendship is that κοινὰ τὰ τῶν φίλων — everything is held in common by friends.[12] This suggests that friendship is based on a sense of solidarity. We must not be led astray by the sound of the word "friendship" into thinking that it conjures up the beauty of some bygone state of spiritual life. The opposite is the case. Life together can be established on no other basis than binding solidarities. Thus all loss of solidarity signifies the suffering of isolation, and, conversely, solidarity always already presupposes what the Greeks called "friendship with oneself," which is brought about, as was shown above, by valuing solitude, and made possible by the capacity to be contentedly alone. In our word "solitude," there is certainly also a suggestion of our fending off the soulless machine of civilization, and a suggestion of sympathy with nature that knows nothing of the human vices. That is the connotation that Rousseau bestowed on the word "solitude." But what the Greeks called friendship — and also precisely what they called friendship with oneself — retains a deep truth.

Plato founded his whole design for a utopian state on the idea that it should be a replica of the soul on a larger scale.[13] The peculiar construction of the state that he describes, with its arrangement of three fixed classes and its class of guardians whose insight steers the destiny of the whole, claims to illustrate what the human soul is and can be. His idea of a constitution that rules out inner discord and binds all the members of the state together in solidary action mirrors the human soul's ability to master its own internal divisions, despite all its conflicts and pent-up urges, and to unite behind one thing. Man's inner constitution and his ability to be part of a community are fundamentally one. Only someone who is friends with himself can fit into what is common.

We are familiar with the case of somebody who is anti-social in the narrow psychiatric sense of the word. He is characterized precisely by the fact that his being intimate with himself and his living together with himself, his unity with himself, has slipped away and broken into pieces. Thus "friendship" here means a fundamental constitution of humanity, that I might call (with Hegel) "being at home with oneself."[14] It is not only today that young people have started rebelling against the way their elders are "at home with themselves." Things were similar when we were young. We saw being too homey with bourgeois society as a loss of freedom and idealism. Nevertheless, friendship with oneself is not tied to this external form of smugly being at home with oneself. Rather, it is the basis of an experience of freedom that we can still achieve today without stooping to a conformism of which we disapprove. I would remind you that in work man is able to find a sense of his own. Even when we feel the compulsions of modern civilization and its mounting pressure, work, and the consciousness of one's own ability that is formed as a result of it, signifies a mysterious form of freedom. I for one think that the consciousness of one's ability is the only form of freedom that can be safely preserved in the face of all the compulsions of our world.

Hegel saw this with wonderful clarity in his famous chapter on lordship and bondage.[15] There he shows that it is not the master but the servant who possesses true self-consciousness, not because he keeps the master enchained to his enjoyment and so is or could be his master's master, but because the servant always already possesses a higher self-consciousness— namely, the consciousness of his own ability—than the master who is dependent on his servitude. In his ability to work, he finds a sense of himself that could not be communicated by the parasitic relation to pleasure enjoyed by the master.

Thus as Hegel rightly saw, the servile consciousness, because it is conscious of the freedom bestowed by its ability, is on the way to a self-consciousness that is more genuinely human than is the master's proud self-consciousness. Now, in the consciousness of freedom that arises from ability, which is the only grounded self-consciousness, individual being is always surpassed by what is common. Ability founds solidarity. Solidarity in ability, responsibility in one's profession, and the knowledge that I share with others and allow others to control, are all forms of solidarity that refer back to the one inherent, fundamental possibility that man has of aligning himself with, or even of making friends with, himself and the world, by working. The untranslatable Greek expression for this phenomenon is "friendship with oneself." It has nothing to do with self-love or egotism: actually, it means the exact opposite. Someone who is not friends with himself, but at odds with himself, is just not fit for any devotion to anyone else, or for any solidarity. It seems that the most profound basis for the self-alienation that we see spreading through modern civilized life lies here, but so also does our inalienable opportunity to conduct our business with the conscious sense of self; in this activity alone do we possess a consciousness of genuine knowledge and genuine ability, in the midst of modern society's undisguisable forms of compulsion. Only in this way can the fate of modern civilization that specialization promotes, instead of ushering in self-alienation, represent the possibility of aligning ourselves with the universal and mediate our social conditionedness with our own consciousness of life.

9

Man and His Hand in Modern Civilization

PHILOSOPHICAL ASPECTS

As the process of civilization marches on around us, the conditions within which we work are changing more and more. No longer can it be assumed that even the most inspired creative ideas will get converted into industrial production, when the whole way in which we communicate with one another has been incorporated, through our technologically organized mass media, into the process of industrialization. Economic interests lead to cheap production and the imitation of already available designs being justified and enforced in the name of business "rationality" (*Rationalität*). No false romantic nostalgia can help us now. We must come to terms with this reality, keeping a practical eye out for the positive possibility that it offers.

It all comes down to the problem of being human. The first thing we assume here is that our senses need to be cultivated (die Sinne sich bilden müssen), and this includes the idea that man must cultivate himself. In this context we sometimes use a word borrowed from the Latin and say that man requires "culture." Man's need to cultivate himself clearly distinguishes him from the rest of the animal kingdom, where we observe an easily acquired mastery of motions and behaviors. Man needs to form himself into something (sich zu etwas bilden), because he is not equipped with that wonderful instinctive certainty that nature has bestowed upon the animals, allowing them to

A lecture given in Munich, 15 February 1978.

orient themselves to the goals of the species: self-preservation and the furthering of life. We humans have thoughts, doubts, and choices about what we should form ourselves into. And this in turn means that we use criteria of evaluation that make rational choice possible for us.

All these realities indicate man's unique situation. By contrast to the demoniacal impulses of our animal instincts, the human spirit is faced with a specific impotence: because we think rather than just act instinctively, we are constantly dealing with possibilities and playing with possibilities. Clearly, the problem of man is this: how can we find a balance that fulfills the law of our nature when we are just as much sensuous creatures as moral ones, just as pervaded and governed by natural instincts as moved by the motivating and supervising power of our ideas? We are obviously defined by something more than just self-preservation, something that includes the whole of human culture, history, progress, regression, decline, recovery, and re-establishment, and everything that makes human history so exemplary and so tragic for every reflective person.

What is at the bottom of this? How are we to find the right orientation, a human balance between the sensuous and moral aspects of our nature? Biologists and anthropologists —for example, Friedrich Nietzsche[1] or in our time Arnold Gehlen[2]—have come to the conclusion that the natural equipment distinctive of humans is our non-specialization. Modern evolutionary theory and paleontology show us how nature is always trying to produce more and more kinds of specialization. One species starves because it can no longer reach down to the ground with its neck, another proves unable to adapt to changed climatic conditions, as with the mammoth. In contrast, it is the distinguishing mark of man to be so unspecialized as to be endowed with a fantastic, virtually unlimited capacity to adapt. If we want to grasp the crisis to which the process of human civilization has led us, we must see the opportunities and the dangers that our human non-specialization brings.

With this in mind, we have every reason to consider the hand. As Aristotle's famous aphorism puts it, the hand is the tool of all tools.[3] This should not be understood in an empty comparative sense, as if Aristotle wanted to say that the hand is a much better tool than all other tools. It means more than that. This part of the body is not itself a tool—it serves no specific ends—but it has the ability to fashion other things to serve as its tool-kit for whatever ends it chooses. So the hand is an intellective organ, a limb that serves for many things and makes many things serve it.

That is why this part of the body is so closely linked with language. The hand not only makes and handles things, it also points to things. There is even a language of the hands: like the human voice, the hand is an organ of communication, which also involuntarily expresses certain things about the person. The whole person is embodied in the hand in the same way that the whole universe of human experience of the world is embodied in language. Together the hand and the speaking voice represent the highest perfection of human non-specialization.

This brings us into a whole new domain, beyond animal self-preservation and beyond nature-the-artist's inexhaustible play of forms. The clever, deliberate creations of free human being bring a constant surplus into human life: play, imitation, rite, ceremony, and all those things that, unnecessary as they are stimulating, we call the beautiful. This is obviously a list that could be extended further, and it enumerates the opportunities that follow from the non-specialization of being human.

But our characteristic lack of specialization also has its dangers. That man has a universal capacity for culture and cultivation means at the same time that he can fall into a kind of artificial specialization. He lacks the stable equilibrium of a sound, healthy animal that uses its instincts and senses to survive. Our human abilities give us innumerable possibilities quite different from this kind of natural balance, but they are possibilities determined by specialization—by work and so always by dividing up work and a process of the division of labor. This now brings us to a whole new dimension of being human, to the social constitution that is peculiar to humanity.

I am not going to discuss what forms of order can successfully fashion the basic political constitution of human life. It is sufficient to make clear how the specialized abilities at our disposal inevitably make us all dependent. The modern world has managed to achieve so astonishingly much through its ability and its genius that it has learned, with the help of science and its technical application, to control and use the forces of nature to an ever greater extent; for just this reason, it views and treats the individual person only as fulfilling a function within the whole of a rational system. The individual stands in a functional context that allows him less and less creative freedom. As a result of our whole cultural process, the individual finds himself more and more in the service of functions, circumscribed by functioning robots and machines. Instead of having the kind of control over things allowed by abilities, which leaves space for the creative play of self-expression, a new kind of universal slavery has come over mankind.

We have to view this slavery as an inescapable fate: man must serve (bedienen) in a functional role. It may be that people of today no longer have to serve (dienen)—i.e., serve other people—but, paradoxically, they must now serve (bedienen) the buttons and levers of the mechanisms that control industrial and agricultural production. With this development, all our human capabilities lose their equilibrium, as does the balance that seems so natural between instinct and intellect, between the way the world limits us and the freedoms it allows us in shaping it. We should be under no illusion: it is science that most deeply determines this contemporary form of human existence.

The enormous estimation that our culture accords to science is nobody's fault or mistake. Science is the most productive factor in our economy and without the continuing productive development of science, without scientific developments and their ingenious technical applications, we can neither maintain the standard of our own civilization nor look forward to improved living conditions for mankind as a whole. We need to see how the hand can coexist with calculation. Calculation, not so much intellect, mind, or understanding, is the omnipotent power organizing our lives. It is what is underneath the complete mediation of our life by industrial civilization: no one even knows the calculations his own hand-outs depend on, which is what makes life so unsatisfactory and so unintuitive.

What about a balance, then? Both sides must obviously be cultivated. Losing a hand means a loss in cultivated senses, but we saw that it is the person himself that needs to be cultivated, his understanding as well as his senses. So the way man is determined and structured confronts him from his cradle on with both resignation and freedom: on the one hand, there is the asceticism of work with its renunciation of the immediate satisfaction of desires, even to the point of renouncing all insight into one's own activity in a world of work that has become alien; and on the other hand. there is the insatiable longing to recognize oneself in the world and to become at home in a world that one has oneself formed.

Thus there is no genuine opposition between intellect and the senses. The hand is an intellective organ, and our senses display their own intelligence insofar as they are inspired by the hand that can touch, grasp, and point as if by freedom. The senses have a certain intelligence, an openness that defends itself against instinctive biases, uncontrolled prejudice, emotional distortion, and indiscriminate inundation by the flood of stimulation. Cultured senses: that ultimately means developing the human capacity for choice and judgment. But the reverse holds true as well—the sensory quality of intelligence. Intelligence is like an unspecialized sense, like the skin that feels everything, an extreme of receptivity and sensitivity. What we call mind or intelligence or reason (*Vernunft*) is a truly universal capacity to understand things, and is in no way limited to the arithmetical arts, measuring procedures, and the tasks of calculation that are so indispensable for technical rationality (Rationalität). If reason (Vernunft) were no more than that, nothing would be able to save us from suffocating mandarins who would give us omnipotent bureaucracy and stagnating progress in technology and civilization.

But what does it mean, we ask, to cultivate one's senses and intelligence? Cultivating (Bilden) is not making. Thus cultivation is closely tied to the conception of the end for which something has been cultivated, so that it is now a such-and-such. Hence cultivation cannot mean developing particular capabilities into proficiencies. Being capable of correctly following a production procedure by pressing a button at the right moment is certainly also a capability and a proficiency that needs to be laboriously learned and thoroughly mastered. But when it comes to cultivation, this possibility of developing one's capabilities is not at issue—it has to do with being in such a way as to make meaningful use of one's capabilities. So cultivation is not to be confused with acquiring proficiencies. Proficiencies are necessary things, and our education should certainly also develop the capabilities of our senses in a rational way, much more than is the case in a school system controlled by the political and economic interests of industrial society. But if such development of proficiencies is to constitute a person's cultivation, so that he becomes a cultivated man with cultivated senses, there must obviously be something else involved: distance from his own abilities and from his own biases and his self-awareness of his own abilities. For someone has cultivated senses only if he is able to see with the sensibility of the whole of his nature, to be observant, notice other things and enter into them.

This sensory cultivation leading to cultivated sensibility is not just an incidental characteristic that might perhaps, under the right circumstances, ripen into special giftedness or real artistic achievements. Artists are fine as they are. But there also have to be people who really need and want their artworks, and that requires a cultivated sensibility. We call this the cultivation of taste: this includes cultivation to the point where one has one's own capacity of judgment. We know how difficult that is. Imitation, mimicry, and fashion reign.

In modern universities, people learn the same way as at school. Future teachers, doctors, and lawyers are examined on the basis of their memory and their formal intellectual proficiency. The university gives them preparatory schooling in theory. Their real education begins only when they begin to practice. To me, our educational system seems somewhat backward, in that students' theoretical preparation excludes them for far too long from participating in the various practical activities of the professions and careers to which they aspire. It's an old problem — how can we diminish the gulf between theoretical academic education and real practical education in such a way that people who want to be, say, teachers, don't simply have to put aside what they've learned at university when they start their teacher training in order to use the favorite books of whoever is organizing the course, who naturally prefers the books that he or she studied as a student? This is obviously the counterpart of the problem we find with theoretical university education: that the ensuing real, practical education does not lead in its turn to "Bildung," but is just a kind of breaking-in.

On both sides, the system (although not necessarily any particular individuals) lacks an awareness of what Bildung really is. Bildung requires and enables one to see things through the eyes of others. Wherever it holds sway, it prevents the particular kinds of one-sidedness that go with school practice, the knowledge gained at college, the mere talent for copying, and the pure training of memory.

This seems to be the current significance of training one's senses, and we must obviously consider the socio-political consequences of reinstating a genuine equilibrium between our sensuous and moral powers. The salient distinguishing feature of art and of the beautiful was that these things are not brought about by mere application of rules, nor is that how one understands them. Art and the beautiful oblige us to use our own judgment. When we consider something beautiful, that in itself means we are ourselves making a judgment. It may be that we often deceive ourselves by just imitating and repeating instead of trusting our own senses and their judgment, but even then this imitating and repeating still follows somebody who really means to judge for themselves, and in the end everybody considers themselves called upon to judge.

This is the great head-start that sensory cultivation and the claim of art offer us in attempting to humanize our lives in our state, society, and administration. Little has fundamentally changed since Schiller hoped aesthetic education would give us a way of progressing toward freedom from the soulless mechanism of the state apparatus.[4] The task before us is still the same. Our capacity for judgment is limited because we are biased by our interests and prejudiced opinions, by our traditions and revolutions, as well as by the whole organized practice of mass manipulation. The automatism of our entire civilized life no longer so easily permits us to feel that we have judgment or that we must credit ourselves with judgment. The high value that the modern working world places on the asceticism that makes specialist skills a duty for the individual leads only too easily to the renunciation of individual judgment in favor of a judgment that is common to all. But then what politically free ways of ordering our lives remain? Only if we think and judge for ourselves about social and political questions and about all the decisions of our own life-experience, despite knowing our limitations and biases, can we hope that the elected political powers — the legislators and the governments that they set up — might also be capable of real cultivated judgment. For in order to hit upon the decisions they have to make, they require the broad resonance of a social whole whose members are willing to use judgment and are capable of critique as well as approval.

10

The Expressive Force of Language
ON THE FUNCTION OF RHETORIC IN
GAINING KNOWLEDGE

In modern civilization the topic of rhetoric is no longer what it was at its ancient origin, nor is it the same as the "rhetoric" that has attended our cultural tradition for so many centuries. For us, the change has to do with converting the art of talking into the art of writing and the art of reading. Talking is talking always to someone or in the presence of someone. This is definitive of the art of talking, but it applies equally to the art of writing and reading that follows from it. For writing too is writing always for someone, however indefinite the addressee may be.

This at once makes clear a problem hidden behind this whole range of topics: the dissociation of writing and reading, which brings about a fundamental modification of understanding. How to bridge the distance between the meaning fixed by the writer and that understood by the reader is the basic question of hermeneutics. For modernity, this is also its pre-eminent problem. I have myself contributed several investigations[1] to showing how the theory of understanding, that is the theory of reading, arises not just on its own but also from the theory of rhetoric. Philip Melanchthon's "Rhetoric," that famous Wittenberg lecture that is printed in three books in the *Corpus Reformatum*,[2] passes silently, as it were, from the basic rhetorical question of composing speeches to the basic hermeneutic ques-

A lecture on the general theme of "scholarly prose," given in Wolfen-büttel in 1979.

tion of understanding the construction of what is written, and so to reading. It cannot be sufficiently emphasized that today what is at issue is not speakers but writers. Here, in literary aesthetics, I believe, lie many as yet unsurmounted problems. Note that there is not only a distinction between a pre-literary civilization and a literary one, but also between a style of writing that produces texts that lend themselves to being read aloud and one that produces them for silent reading. I believe these are problems that we shall have to incorporate into our aesthetics of style in a way quite different from what has hitherto been the case.

I am a bit of a classical philologist; so for me the connection between rhetoric and writing is an old Platonic problem. I recall here that Plato's quarrel with rhetoric has two sides. For him, rhetoric is not merely what it is in our general consciousness, where it has acquired a somewhat pejorative connotation—the art of flattery that can talk anyone into anything without any sincere conviction or relationship to the truth. Above all in the Gorgias, Plato made us aware of this once and for all in that famous comparison between rhetoric and cookery. But in the Phaedrus, he also said that rhetoric can sometimes stand in an essential relation to finding and communicating insight and knowledge.[3] I believe Plato displayed great insight in showing that true rhetoric is not to be divided from what he calls "dialectic," dialectic in that originary sense that comprises the art of conducting a conversation.[4] In the end, the art of conducting a conversation is the art of coming to an understanding. Thus, understanding ultimately turns out to be mutual understanding and takes place in this communicative context of coming to a complete understanding with one another. Now it is, I think, a crucial insight of Plato's, attesting to his wisdom, that dialectic presupposes good-will.[5] The Greek expression for this is *eumenia*. Plato uses it to refer to the concrete situation of mutual understanding as opposed to blindly rigorous argument; it is the intent to come to an understanding that first gives discourse its true possibility and, so to speak, opens up the way to insight.

This reminder lets us see the new task of rhetoric. It is quite plain that it requires an art of writing, because all the means and possibilities of understanding one another that can be mustered in dialogue and conversation must be given up in view of the dissociation of what is written from what the reader is to understand. The word "prose" itself indicates this. We can all agree that nobody would speak of "prose" if there were no verse. Prose is a hermeneutic concept. The word suggests that there is still an art of language when a text is not constitutively bound in metrical feet but walks, as it were, directly along the footpath of the thought. Thus the art of prose had in fact already become a topic of discussion in antiquity. Our main source is Dionysius of Halicarnassus, who described the great writers of histories—the great historians—as models of style superior to any of the great speakers, that is, the great speech writers.[6] Our concept of style and its refinement stems from this reflection on the art of writing.

I now turn to the theme that has emerged in our civilization, marked as it is by modern science, in reference to writing clearly and writing well. It is clear that initially modernity was directly tied to its ancient heritage. Humanism embraced the ideal of *imitatio*, the emulation of the rhetorical and stylistic art of classical antiquity, which viewed Roman and Greek achievements as almost seamlessly one. A change occurred when book printing, and the aftermath of the Reformation, ushered in the beginning of silent reading. This fact is fundamental. To be sure, the rhetorical continuity with antiquity was preserved, especially in Protestant forms of worship, in the art of preaching. But now silent reading came to be a powerful counterpoise. Into this situation stepped the great revolution of the seventeenth century. It cannot be denied that the new empirical science with its new ideal of method, applying mathematical projections to nature and natural processes, brought a new tension into the world between language and knowledge. It is clear—and one cannot penetrate this question deeply enough—that at bottom the concept of an empirical science has paradoxical connotations for the tradition from which our civilization developed. Science that needs only experience in order to be true! What kind of "science" is that? Mathematics was the uncontested science of antiquity. In mathematics, truth is established from concepts through thought's own self-development. As soon as experience comes into it, science can be effective only in a supporting role. And now modernity turns everything upside down. To this day, mathematics does not know where it fits in. It has no place whatever among the natural sciences and the human sciences. Nor does it claim to have one, though it knows it is the only uncontested science of reason. But by the word "science" we now quite self-evidently understand empirical science. "There can be no doubt that all our knowledge begins with experience"—so runs the first sentence of the *Critique of Pure Reason*.[7] And this becomes the new theme: how can the new cognitive tasks of modern science be reconciled with the tradition of cultivation and knowledge that is carried forward by rhetoric? Clearly this question represents a thus far unresolved and, I am convinced, also irresolvable tension.

But though this tension sometimes obliges us to study the art of writing as researchers, it obliges us to it just as inexorably in making our thinking accurate and communicating its results. To illustrate how this tension still survives, I need only point out that the rhetorical interpretation of the world still rules everywhere in spite of Galileo and Copernicus. The sun still always goes down for us (as it so obviously did for pre-Copernican astronomy). We do not say "the earth turns away."

This illustrates the way language can detach itself from the scientific ways of explaining phenomena. It can survive in this separation because it has its own orientation to and articulation of the world.

If we consider this fact, we shall at once be clear that language must in principle take on new tasks for modern empirical science. The mathematical model of nature implied that the laws of free-fall or an inclined plane must be mathematically formulable regardless of the nature of the falling bodies and the postulate of concrete observability. As is well known, Galileo formulated these laws before a vacuum existed, and so before anyone could have observed what today we see in the classroom: that in a vacuum a bed-feather falls just as fast as a lead plate. Precisely by means of this mathematicizing model, he defined a new concept—the "object" (*des Objektes, des Gegenstandes*)—whereas before there was no such word or thing. "Object" or "Gegenstand" is defined through a "method" that prescribes how reality gets made into an object. The aim of methodically researching the object in this way is then essentially to break down the resistance of "objects" and to dominate the processes of nature; the basic intentions of technology are certainly not conscious, but they are an immanent consequence of it, and their reality surrounds us on all sides in the shape of our technological civilization.

This reality presents a new task for language. Because of the constructive character of the modern knowledge of nature, language has to give up its position of linguistic totality, so to speak, and limit itself to specific designatory functions. This is already evident in the beginnings of European science. For example, Johannes Lohmann has shown in a beautiful work called *Musike und Logos* (Stuttgart, 1970) that certain concepts in mathematics and geometry are entirely artificial re-coinings of words—metaphors, which, modern semantics would say, have become dead metaphors. The Greek expression for a geometrical angle is "knee," *gony*, but no mathematician thought he was saying "knee" because what he was talking about was a new reality constituted by Euclidean mathematics, which otherwise did not exist. Thus it was concerned with adequately designating a well-defined concept, and no longer to do with a "word." The ideal language of mathematics has in a certain sense reduced the function of language to designation, so that we no longer use language in the way Aristotle had in mind in that famous definition of what distinguishes man from the animals. There he says that man has language not so that we can give signals to one another as birds give one another warning and mating signals, but in such a way that we have the logos, the language that consists in *delun* (revealing), in making the real states of affairs manifest. That means that we do not merely point to something but also recognize it for what it is.

Now this, clearly, is the life-world of language: it is itself an interpretation of the life-world. This expression—"life-world" (*Lebenswelt*)—is one of those rare successful philosophical words. It is an expression of Husserl's that in the last few decades has, so to speak, found a way into the Germans' sense of language. In this word the life-world takes cognizance of itself in opposition to the scientific world of objects defined by the methodical attainment of knowledge.

Now, this life-world component has patently all along been at the bottom of what I have designated as the rhetorical tradition of antiquity and of the Middle Ages. What rhetoric as such is based on is a kind of common language, the language of our common sense, our sensus communis.[8] This can be seen in the example of Freud's early prose[9] or perhaps Theodor Mommsen's history of Rome.[10] Both examples belong completely under the rubric of rhetoric. This means that they are formulated using the values of a universally accepted common sense that can be used for describing objects or events just as they present themselves to the researcher. Yet, the greatness of a great researcher like Freud, who discovered a new dimension of depth to the mental, or a great researcher like Mommsen, who could discern the seeds of nineteenth-century bourgeois culture in the ancient Roman republic, lies altogether elsewhere.

It should certainly not be forgotten that in Freud's language there is a significant level of interference between the concepts he forms and the living force of language: without doubt his survey of the new dimension of the unconscious is dominated by particular scientific ways of presenting things, which require well-defined concepts. Nevertheless, the linguistic context that surrounds his concepts betrays the fact that he is a master of scholarly prose. And again, Mommsen, that great researcher, is obviously fully justified in bringing the rhetorical component provided by sensus communis into his characterization of historical knowledge. In just this way he reveals, and we discern, that all of this is continuous with the great historical process of coming to an understanding in which men try to understand one another. Here too, the art of coming to an understanding ultimately remains the crucial component, at least within the group of sciences that we call the humaniora, and perhaps not just there. Grammatically, "humaniora" is a comparative form. This might provoke a great deal of thought, as much about the positive that makes all science human as about the superlative that no science can quite attain.

Were I to summarize these considerations, I might begin by bringing to our attention a few plain and trivial facts: there is, of course, a language of science. Rhetoric demands that one know to and for whom one is speaking. It was a great insight of Plato's that the use of rhetorical means, rousing the emotions with moving forms of style and speech, can definitely be used in the service of acquiring knowledge. Thus it is no doubt best to address any particular circle of research groups in the way that will enable those research groups to best grasp what is being communicated. To research is to continue the dialogue by other means. For this reason, even the most eminent researchers often prefer publishing a few pages in a journal that change the world to writing long books. There is a dialogue in the specialist academic periodicals. What filters through from this dialogue into the textbooks (which have their own aesthetics and dialectics) again has its own form of rhetoric that I do not want to overlook. But it presents the challenge of stopping this kind of summary of research from entering scientific usage as new dogma. We can ultimately define a researcher as someone who is familiar with what the textbooks say but does not believe it. That is a really sound principle. But we are still faced with the task of developing the specifics of textbook rhetoric so that the provisional nature of our knowledge and our openness to the progress of research are made effective in the reader's understanding.

The real theme to which this reflection is dedicated, scholarly prose, certainly means something different. "Scholarly prose" cannot really be defined as "scientific prose." The expression "scholarly prose," which sounds a little less refined, reminds us that now, in the twentieth century, a decided change separates us from the culture of the eighteenth century. The young scholar was also a theme of Gotthold Lessing's, and he certainly brought out the humor of it.[11] Today it no longer takes a Lessing to do that. I remember one time when I was ill and was asked in the clinic what I was, I said: a "scholar." (You can see from this how strangely confined was the life-world of a young academic in my own youth.) My medical friends, I believe, could hardly stop laughing.

The change to which I refer is the linguistic one that has taken place between the eighteenth century's "scholar," the nineteenth's "researcher," and today's "scientist," a change that sheds a good deal of light on our conception of ourselves. It is echoed in the antiquated phrase "scholarly prose." This is not to question the fact, which doubtless cannot be altered if research is to go forward, that progress always has to choose the most economical way of communicating knowledge, and so of carrying on discussion within research. On the other hand, whenever one is concerned about having a continuing claim to intelligibility, the word "scholarly" is a very appropriate label to use. "Scholarly prose" means that here someone is speaking who has mastered a science and yet is capable of making himself so intelligible to uneducated (*ungelernt*) people—uneducated is the true opposite of "scholarly" (*gelehrt*)[12]—that they learn something. This is an "art" needed in science as well as in literature. It seems to have its external expression in, for example, the fact that books (and not just textbooks, those continuations of the dialogue by another means that constitute the immanent process of science) are written to indefinite addressees and possible readers, and are written by writers who know that they have to lead an indeterminate number of people, who are not participating in the actual classroom dialogue, down a path toward understanding and penetration into the subject matter. This necessitates keeping a certain distance from things that are familiar to us. If we want to speak as scholars and still be intelligible to the uneducated, we must renew in ourselves the old virtues of dialectic and rhetoric. The distance involved here is not to be confused with the distancing that is demanded by the scientific method, which consists in alienation from a world of objects and overcoming this alienation by exploration and scientific explanation. The art of scholarly prose has to do with another kind of distance—distance from oneself. Its job is to achieve a particular kind of mediation between one's own knowledgeability and the reader's lacking it. This, it seems, is the real essence of scholarly prose—that it consciously takes on and exercises this function of mediation. It is not surprising, then, that it has a much greater scope in the human sciences, the non-historical social sciences, and the linguistic sciences. It is enlightening to note that it is not by chance that linguists are bad stylists. What unnatural reflections about language-as-such are demanded of them! They are supposed to make language into an object, rather than the things that are communicated through language.

We are not primarily oriented toward language in our lives. Nor are we primarily oriented toward fine language.

We should keep this firmly in mind when thinking about "scholarly prose"—namely, that what distinguishes scholarly prose is its being wholly motivated by the things it communicates. We should not be tempted to distinguish between what is really being said and communicated and the fine "way" it is said. The great artistic metaphors that we admire in the great stylists and essayists do not testify as such to the art of scholarly prose. To use an example: a very precious and elegant passage from Walter Benjamin makes sense to me because the book in question is a good one,[13] but not because this phrase as such is a good example of scholarly prose. It has its rhetorical and stylistic function. It puts the reader in a particular mood and perhaps in that way facilitates accepting the research results. It could be the evocative power of such emotive language that invites Benjamin to use these precious turns of phrase in describing bourgeois tragic drama from the point of view of its Jesuit background—I read Benjamin's book a long time ago and am no expert on it. But without a doubt, that is not the language of scholarly prose. It is only the first step toward developing one's own laws of style. Since Plato's *Nomoi* (Laws), we have known something about this law of style.[14] But this kind of linguistic art is to be properly distinguished from concern with the matter under discussion that is the aim of scholarly prose as a whole.

Certainly we should not forget what an irresolvable tension there is between modern science's concept of method and the desire for sympathetic understanding we have as people who live in the world. Modern science's concept of method demands that boundaries be set. What is attainable by method defines what can be an object for exploration. From this, it follows necessarily that research is one particular approach to reality, and it is for just this reason that pragmatic devices are appropriate to secure this approach—codifications, mathematical symbolisms, artificial logic, or whatever. But I need only mention these symbolizations to call attention to the fact that not even a natural researcher can completely communicate what he thinks by these means alone. He cannot wholly free himself from the life-world and its linguistic articulation. It is very true that this can lead to misunderstandings. I remember (I did not really understand this until today) that my late Heidelberg colleague and friend Hans Jensen[15] had read a work of mine[16] in which I said something (and I think, in itself, the right thing) about the concept of force in Herder and Hegel and its connection with Newton. He responded, "Yes, but that has nothing in the least to do with the concept of force in physics." That is precisely the point. In this instance, a scientific concept of force has become so dissociated from the concept of force in the mother tongue with all its evocative power that the use of the word can be a source of misunderstanding and false simplifications, misleading apparent understanding, adherence to prejudices, and the like. In everyday language as well as in the so-called Geisteswissenschaften ("human sciences"), everything that increases speech's rich variety of reference and extends its capacity for containing knowledge can turn into confusion when everything depends on univocal denotation. The metaphorical nature of language makes definition necessary and justifies the use of artificial terminology. This cannot be introduced by means of wholly determinate language alone, but only through natural speech. The comparative particularity of scientific languages as they dissociate themselves within the overall phenomenon of language always stands in tension with the totality that binds us all together into a human society, our ability to speak, to seek and find words to communicate.

In honor of Lessing, who is very much in our thoughts this year,[17] I conclude with a quotation from him. We know that Lessing was not exactly a great advocate of mystical, inexact, or irrational modes of thinking. And yet we find the following sentence in a work where he is criticizing someone's overly one-sided concept of science. Lessing says it is "something that dries up the wits and accustoms them to a physical precision that has nothing in common with the metaphysical precision of poets and speakers."

II

Good German

One can only learn from examples. This is an old truth, though few may welcome it in our age of hurtling Enlightenment, which takes such pleasure in experiment and construction. This truth is never so convincing and unavoidable as when we are dealing with language, with speaking, and with writing. Now, language certainly seems to be all rules and conventions, and it might seem that using speech and writing freely and independently is possible only by completely mastering all its obligatory conventions and rules. Where rules reign, though, there can be no examples.

But there is something peculiar about rules—about the rules of language, of spelling and punctuation, and perhaps many others that govern our behavior. Is our behavior really governed just by the application of rules? Or do they not rather constitute a dead framework of rectitude whose life is revealed to us in the exceptions, the deviations, and the ventures beyond what is correct and regular? Think how hard it is—how unnatural, even—to render at all explicit the system of rules of one's own mother tongue. Our language sense is much more at home with replying, and it perceives rules, even if it upholds and "follows" them, as an unnecessary abstraction. Grammar may be very helpful to those learning foreign languages, but even then it is not the most natural way of learning. Most important, what writer, even one with the modest claim to greatness

A speech of acceptance given in Darmstadt in October 1979 on receiving the "Sigmund Freud Prize" from the German Academy for Language and Poetry.

that we ascribe to a scholar, does not sometimes find that his style is cramped by the rules of language and grammar, established vocabulary, spelling, and punctuation? Who has not lost the battle against Duden[1] and the copyeditor countless times by being unwise enough not to risk going beyond them?

And who really learned to write at school anyway? We reject its essay style and that frightful translator's German that one tends to make do with for didactic reasons. When we learn the way we do at school, it is always difficult to preserve what little room for play is allowed us by the conventions of language governing our speaking and writing, and in the end we have to defend ourselves less from these linguistic norms themselves than from the compulsory stylistic model that our teachers' authority represents. This goes for schools of all levels, including universities.

Or am I talking about a bygone age of authoritarian education, and an equally bygone age in which one's sense of language and perception of style would slowly grow from and beyond examples, feeding on the treasures of one's own memory—the German of the Lutheran bible and a rich and artistic repertoire of poetic language? Has the new ubiquity of the mass media's oily rhetoric allowed modern man's linguistic imagination to dry out, especially now that we view learning by heart as repression?

But no. The antagonism between rhetoric and linguistic creativity has existed all along. It is as true today as it always was that you can learn to write only if you feel free (on this we can surely all agree), and you feel free only if you choose your examples and models for yourself. How can you even think of speaking or writing under the illusion that you're the first person ever to speak or write? Everything that language can do, the forms and arrangements that words allow and the thoughts they invite us to, those "cunning, bird-voiced daughters" (to quote this year's winner of the Büchner Preis)[2]—none of this is stored in a warehouse like raw material for some indeterminate and arbitrary purpose. Instead, it occupies a space in which there is a constant play back and forth between what has already been said and what is still to be said, between choices already made and still to be made. Of course, the poets are boldest of all, and for the most part we unknowingly follow their adventurous spirit in applying words and turns of phrase. Adopting models in speaking or writing is not primarily a conscious choice, since speaking and writing themselves consist, after all, not so much in choosing words as in following their invitations. Yet language is wise enough to speak of "turns of phrase," of *tropoi*—these are paths that language has beaten for itself which, as such, recommend themselves to new applications. In this respect, freedom is at the same time both a further solidification and a new yielding, a turning away from a former way of speaking and a turning toward another, new direction of saying.

But this very reliance on ready-made language and adopted models—as well as the way what has already been said is followed in subsequent speech and writing—can, on the other hand, seduce us into those inaccurate, thoughtless, approximate things we call "clichés" (*Redensarten*), "mere clichés" that are more or less expressly opposed to careful discourse that can answer for what it says. This negative, deadening effect of ready-made language makes itself felt even when we think we are being productive. For a creative writer, to imitate is to fail himself by lapsing into the tone of his models. The leveling influence of what has already been said and written, then, is especially effective on everyone who speaks in a merely imitative way, as we all do when we talk, and everyone does who can write but is not a poet. Still, it does credit to the prose of our thought that it is wholly dedicated to communicating what it is thinking, and all its efforts go into bringing out the thought rather than one's own artistic style.

And so we see the situation of a man of science. He is supposed to write well, but he does not submit to any rigid norm, be it orthodox correctness, a particular stylistic model, or any conscious stylistic ideal. There is no fixed norm of scientific speech and writing. Anyone who has considered the French in this regard knows that they put greater stock in style and hold it in much higher esteem than we do. The scholarly prose that unites narrative *histoire naturelle* with *littérature,* which Buffon not only demanded but himself exemplified in the eighteenth century, remained flexible and so was vulnerable to the criticisms of the subsequent generation, who saw him as a *parlier.* Yet the truth he captured in his formula "le style c'est l'homme"[3] nevertheless transcends all the contingencies of any particular time. If a scholar's style has not moved beyond all consideration of models or orthodox correctness, if the art of his writing does not operate like his own nature, he has no style, or rather he has not yet attained the freedom to use his own style.

Seeming natural is certainly itself subject to changing times, alterations in ideals of taste and in our sensibilities. The style is the man—but what is the man? Certainly not simply a natural creature that grows to maturity, but someone who forms or cultivates himself, from playful imitations to development by consciously or unconsciously adopting models in speaking and writing. But there are special limits imposed on the man of scientific and scholarly prose. What an artist who works with prose, such as a storyteller, is supposed to do and wants to do, is to make a certain art of writing into a palpable reality. The possibility is open to him of formulating his own style, although, as a style, it will always go unnoticed to some extent. Even a writer who is a journalist and essayist has possibilities of this kind and stands, so to speak, halfway between the poet, for whom a tone of one's own is everything, and the man of science.

But then what is left for the man of science, the scholar? The answer is both simple and hard: That indefinable "good German!" It is an ideal that can hardly be attained by the philosopher. Arthur Schopenhauer's invectives against the German philosophers' lack of down-to-earth readability are well-known,[4] and there is probably no reader who does not have difficulties with the philosophers' German. The elegance and refinement of Immanuel Kant's language is certainly not to be criticized, but we must admit that for all the facility and readability that Kant's style lends to particular details, he does place huge, scarcely fulfillable demands on his reader—especially on his power of concentration and his capacity to follow the rigorous and striking constructs of a true architect of thought. Who would dare to take this style as a model for his own? Johann Fichte's almost showy rhetoric (although his contemporaries attributed his first work to Kant himself when it was published), Friedrich Schelling's charming mixture of dry scholasticism and inspired profundity, or even Hegel's quasi-German with its highly characteristic and unmistakable Swabian tendency to shock—these we might admit are the achievements of great stylists, but we would hardly want to imitate them. As we have seen over the decades, or even centuries, in, say, the many Hegelians of the nineteenth and twentieth centuries, or in the Heideggerian German of philosophy between the wars, the lecture hall appears to demand and produce its own barbarity, and its special power of suggestion is owing to just that.

Moreover, the conditions under which the various forms of knowledge operate play a formative role in scholars' styles. "Lectures" and the publication of big, comprehensive books are not, generally speaking, the central venues of a natural scientist's work, whereas this very often is the case for "humanists;" and that must have its influence on the prose style of scholarly writing in these fields.

Academic rhetoric, then, develops its own formative power, which affects the style of scholarly prose. It may not be easy for somebody to be a good speaker if he is to stand the test of everyday academic life. The rhetoric of the political rostrum or the pulpit is insufferable in the lecture hall. Conversely, good academic speakers who speak in parliament tend to sound as though they are addressing a women's circle. Within the academic métier, the didactic component will always show through, even when one is lecturing in an academic setting about well-styled texts (as Friedrich Gundolf did),[5] and even when one is perfectly clear about the stylistic distinction between good presentation in public speaking and verbal communication of research results.

In both respects, then, teaching and research clearly exert a dangerous influence on those who are supposed to write scholarly prose: the attentive lecture hall and the esoteric research circle have little in common with the reader, who needs to be won over first. So I do not think the question of which models a scientist should choose from among the masters of science, or a philosopher from among the masters of his métier, in order to learn good German, is correctly posed at all.

I will illustrate this point from the history of my own linguistic development: in my day one's first real contact with verbal art was still in learning Latin and reading the speeches of Cicero. Construing and translating long sentences requires adherence to a rule of logical construction over great distances, and this teaches an initial lesson in taking up distance and so gives an initial freedom to one's own usage. How the art of writing and rendering trains of thought accurately can be passed on to a younger generation that has not been through this kind of schooling is, I think, an open question.

The German that was spoken in the middle-class world in my hometown, Breslau, was fairly free of dialect. In those days that was considered an advantage, and it was made particularly important at school. But this language certainly lacked vividness and force, especially as exemplified in the well-to-do newspapers and journals of those years that came into my hands, whose style of writing was as artless as it was lifeless. So it was on the back stairs, in the maid's newspaper, that I came across Walter and Paul Rilla's theater reviews;[6] in their facility and grace I found again something of Gotthold Lessing's prose, which I had long admired. The young Hermann Hesse's polished style or the young Thomas Mann's skillful wording might also have pushed me in the same direction.

But breaking into philosophy, into the language of Kant and neo-Kantianism, and the general strain of lifting the conceptual load with which one is burdened by philosophical studies, demanded an even stronger counterbalance. This came to me above all from the great German lyric poetry that, in my youth, used to echo through the entire space of the German language. Hugo von Hofmannsthal, Stefan George, Rainer Maria Rilke, and Friedrich Hölderlin,[7] whose work was only then beginning to be ranked as world literature, constantly reminded us of the evocative power with which language attests to its own freedom and sovereignty—and what is better able consistently to show philosophical ideas their own task (by which I mean the task of pointing to things that are not there and never have been there) than the language of poetry?

The tragedy of conceptual thinking was vividly demonstrated —to one who was only too familiar with it on his own account —in Hölderlin's prose sketches, those endless self-entangled convolutions of reflection that constantly postpone their goals, conclusions and outcomes, so that in the end one whole page forms a single gigantic antecedent to which the world itself could not provide a counterbalance sufficient in force and significance.[8] Nor did the dark pathways where Heidegger, driven by his questions, beat against the rock of language, lead out into the daylight of common clarity. I could even admire my friend Max Kommerell's artistic style[9] without wanting it to replace the declarative force of conceptual language. I much preferred to let myself be filled instead by the spirit of lightheartedness for which I found Goethe's prose exemplary, and which sometimes seemed to recur in Nietzsche and in the learned variations of Nietzsche's style of that master philologist, my personal friend, Karl Reinhardt.[10] But let me also mention a living person here: Dolf Sternberger, whose prose enlightens by the clarity of its simultaneous precision and nonchalance.[11]

If my path from school exercises to prose instructed by art and ruled by conceptual abstraction, yet still readable, has borne fruit, I have this succession of helpful models to thank. The German Academy for Language and Poetry appointed me to its circle in its very first year and now publicly honors me by associating me with the name of a Sigmund Freud; this might make me believe I have had some success in finding a balance between concept and word, between the art of thinking and teaching and the art of writing. If so, the same might be said in the humble case of scholarly prose: Ars latet arte sua—art hides itself through its own art.[12]

Notes

Lob der Theorie is published in German with no notes at all. In spite of this, Gadamer makes frequent references in all of the essays it contains to works of German and classical literature and philosophy that will not necessarily be familiar to an English speaking reader. I have therefore endeavored to track down the references and include them in these notes.

Gadamer speaks without detailed advanced preparation, and when he quotes he does so from memory. As a result his quotations are not always accurate, so I have included the original versions of the texts to which they refer where these differ from Gadamer's versions.

Gadamer also has a tendency to extract general themes from the corpus of a writer's work, and to refer to these without having any specific passage exclusively in mind. This is especially true in relation to Aristotle, so where I have provided a reference to Aristotle in connection with a remark of Gadamer's, it should not be assumed that that is the only passage he has in mind.

Introduction

1. See his 1947 Rectoral address to the University of Leipzig, "On the Primordiality of Science," in *Applied Hermeneutics*, 15–21.
2. He makes this suggestion tentatively at first on page 14 of *The Idea of the Good in Platonic-Aristotelian Philosophy*.
3. See "Plato's Unwritten Dialectic," in *Dialogue and Dialectic*.
4. The importance of Plato's form of the beautiful for Gadamer's philosophical account can be seen from the work it does at the very end of *Truth and Method*, 487–8.

I
Culture and the Word

1. Jean-Jacques Rousseau, *A Discourse on the Moral Effects of the Arts and Sciences [First Discourse]* (1750), in *The Collected Writings of Rousseau*, trans.

Judith R. Bush, Roger D. Masters, and Christopher Kelly, vol. 2: *Discourse on the Sciences and Arts, and Polemics* (Hanover, N.H., University Press of New England, 1992).

2. Immanuel Kant, *Bemerkungen zu den Beobachtungen über das Gefühl des Schönen und Erhabenen,* posthumously published from a handwritten manuscript, in *Kants gesammelte Schriften herausgegeben von der Preußischen Akademie der Wissenschaften,* vol. 20 (Berlin: Walter de Gruyter, 1942), 44.

3. Johann Gottfried Herder, *Ideen zur Philosophie der Geschichte der Menschheit,* vol. 2 (1791) (Berlin/Weimar: Aufbau, 1965), 38. "Lasset dieses ["Zivilisation eines Volks"] die Stufe einer noch sehr unvollkommenen Kultur sein, sie ist indessen für die Kindheit des Menschengeschlechts notwendig." "Even if this [a people's 'civilization'] is the level of a very incomplete culture, it is still necessary for the childhood of the human race."

4. Arthur Schopenhauer, *The World as Will and Representation* (1819), trans. E. F. J. Payne—2 vols. (New York: Dover Publications/Falcon's Wing Press, 1958).

5. Walter Benjamin, "Das Kunstwerk im Zeitalter seiner technischen Reproduzierbarkeit" in his Gesammelte Schriften, vol. 1.2 (Frankfurt am Main: Suhrkamp, 1974). Translated by Harry Zohn as "The Work of Art in the Age of Mechanical Reproduction" in *Illuminations,* ed. Hannah Arendt (New York: Schocken Books, 1969).

6. Herder, "Älteste Urkunde des Menschengeschlechts" in his *Werke,* vol. 5: *Schriften zum Alten Testament* (Frankfurt am Main: Deutscher Klassiker Verlag, 1993).

7. Genesis 1.3.

8. Friedrich Hölderlin, *Friedensfeier* ("Festival of Peace"), l.92. The line is slightly misquoted (Gadamer inserts "können"). The verse from which it is taken runs:

> Viel hat von Morgen an,
> Seit ein Gespräch wir sind und hören voneinander,
> Erfahren der Mensch; bald sind wir aber Gesang.
> Und das Zeitbild, das der große Geist entfaltet,
> Ein Zeichen liegts vor uns, daß zwischen ihm und andern
> Ein Bündnis zwischen ihm und andern Mächten ist.

> Man has, from morning on,
> Since we are a conversation and hear from one another,

Much experience; but soon we are song.
And the picture of time the great spirit unfolds
Lays a sign before us, that is an alliance it makes
With other powers, between it and others.

9. Ferdinand Ebner, *Das Wort und die geistigen Realitäten: pneumatolo-gische Fragmente*, vol. 1 of his *Gesammelte Werke* (Vienna: Verlag Herder, 1952), 33.

10. Aristotle, *Politics*, 1.2.1253a10.

11. Cf. Martin Heidegger, *Being and Time* (1926), trans. John Macquarrie and Edward Robinson (Oxford: Blackwell, 1962), paragraphs 6 and 7, pp. 47 and 55–58, where he explains his rendering of Aristotle's phrase "*zoon logon echon*" as the living being that can talk rather than as "rational animal." Heidegger gives no reference for the phrase, which does not seem to appear in Aristotle in exactly this form. Aristotle's statement that rationality (tou logon echontos) is the distinguishing feature of man is most clearly stated at *Nichomachean Ethics*, 1.7.1098a1–20.

12. Aristotle, *Politics*, 1253a8–18

13. In the original Greek the last three sentences given here are in fact a single sentence that lasts from the second line to the end of the passage.

14. Op. cit.

15. Aristotle, *De Interpretatione*, chapters 2 and 4, 16a16 and 17a1. "*Kata syntheken*" means "by convention." On convention, see page 59.

16. The third part of *Truth and Method* is a more detailed discussion of the philosophical importance of language.

17. "*Koine sympheron*" means just "useful in common to all."

18. Gadamer is referring to the passage he already quoted above, where the Greek has "to sympheron kai to blaberon, hoste kai to dikaion kai to adi-kon" (of what is helpful and what is harmful and so also of what is right and what is wrong).

19. *Nomos* means "law" and *syntheke* means "convention." Aristotle identifies law as a convention at Politics, 1280b10, and applies this to language at the beginning of De Interpretatione.

20. See *Eudemian Ethics*, 2.2.1220b1–3, where Aristotle suggests that the Greek word ἦθος from which "ethics" is derived, has its origins in the word ἔθος, which means "habit."

21. Plato, *Republic*, 2.368–372

22. 372d5. It is actually Glaucon who makes the comment.

23. See page 16.

24. For more detail on Gadamer's central notion of "the beautiful," see *The Relevance of the Beautiful*, 14 ff.

25. Marcus Tullius Cicero, *Tusculan Disputations*, 2.5.13: "Ut ager quamvis fertilis sine cultura fructuosus esse non potest, sic sine doctrina animus. . . . Cultura autem animi philosophia est." (Just as a field, however fertile it may be, cannot be productive without cultivation, the same is true of the mind without teaching. . . . But the cultivation of the mind is philosophy.)

26. I.e., Aristotle in the passage quoted earlier.

27. See Ernst Cassirer, *An Essay on Man: An Introduction to a Philosophy of Human Culture* (New Haven: Yale University Press, 1944), chapter 2. Gadamer himself makes use of the notion of a symbol in *The Relevance of the Beautiful*, 31-32 and in *Truth and Method*, 72-73.

28. A more detailed explanation of Gadamer's understanding of "tradition" can be found in *Truth and Method*, 280-283.

29. See page 89.

30. Author of the *Tao-te-ching*, and founder of Taoism.

31. Gadamer sees the "dialectic of question and answer" as the fundamental mode of operation not only of philosophy but of language and understanding themselves. See *Truth and Method*, 362-379.

32. Our word "planet" comes from the Greek word *planaomai*, which means to wander.

33. Eduard Mörike, "Auf eine Lampe" ("On a Lamp"):

> Noch unverrückt, o schöne Lampe, schmückest du,
> An leichten Ketten zierlich aufgehangen hier,
> Die Decke des nun fast vergeßnen Lustgemachs.
> Auf deiner weißen Marmorschale, deren Rand
> Der Efeukranz von goldengrünem Erz umflicht,
> Schlingt fröhlich eine Kinderschar den Ringelreihn.
> Wie reizend alles! Lachend und ein sanfter Geist
> Des Ernstes doch ergossen um die ganze Form:
> Ein Kunstgebild der echten Art. Wer achtet sein?
> Was aber schön ist, selig scheint es in ihm selbst.
>
> O lamp so beautiful, unmoved you still adorn
> The wall, suspended daintily on your light chains,
> Of this almost forgotten but once pleasant room.
> On your white marble shell, around the edge of which

An ivy wreath of golden-greenish ore is bound,
Some children, tripping in a merry circle, dance.
How charming it all is! A tender spirit pours
Out, laughing yet in earnest still, round the whole form:
An artwork of the proper kind. Who'll notice it?
What's beautiful, though, shines as if blessed in itself.

34. This sentence contains a reference to Hegel's dialectic. The two German words I have included both derive from the verb *aufheben,* which Hegel uses for the dialectical unification of opposite moments: *Aufhebung* has been variously translated as "synthesis," "sublation," "transcension," and "cancellation." The difficulty is that the word is used in two senses at once: it means both canceling out and raising to a higher level.

2
Praise of Theory

1. "Metic" was the name given to a resident of a Greek city who was not born there and therefore did not have the full rights of citizenship.
2. Gadamer analyzes "play" in great detail in *Truth and Method,* 101–110, and in *The Relevance of the Beautiful,* 22–25 and 123–130.
3. Kant, *Über den Gemeinspruch: Das mag in der Theorie richtig sein, taugt aber nicht für die Praxis,* 1793 (Frankfurt-am-Main: Vittorio Klostermann, 1968).
4. Plato, *Republic,* 7.514–518.
5. See Gadamer's analysis of *Bildung* in *Truth and Method,* 9–19, and also p. 121 of this volume.
6. Aristotle, Nichomachean Ethics, 1.1.1094a1, trans. W. D. Ross and J. O. Urmson, revised by J. Barnes (Revised Oxford Aristotle, 1984). This translation is a fairly literal one, but Gadamer's translation into German is very free. It reads more like "All efforts of knowing, ability and choice have to do with the good."
7. Aristotle, *Metaphysics,* 1.980a1.
8. Pliny the Elder (Gaius Plinius Secundus), *Natural History* (10 vols.), trans. H. Rackham, Loeb Classical Library (London: William Heinemann, 1938 and 1949).
9. In St. Aurelius Augustine, Bishop of Hippo *De Vera Religione,* chapters 49–52. This work is not easy to find in English translation.
10. See page 1.

11. Georg Wilhelm Friedrich Hegel, *Hegel's Philosophy of Mind, Being Part Three of the Encyclopaedia of the Philosophical Sciences* (1830), trans. William Wallace, (Oxford: Clarendon, 1971), 292–315.

12. Karl Marx and Friedrich Engels, *The German Ideology* (1845-r6) Part I-A1, trans. W. Lough, (London: Lawrence and Wishart, 1965), 43–45.

13. Thomas Mann, *Buddenbrooks: The Decline of a Family* (1902), trans. H. T. Lowe-Porter (Harmondsworth: Penguin, 1924). Mann's first novel charts the epic tale of a merchant family's fall from grace amid changes in the society of the nineteenth century.

14. See especially *The World as Will and Representation* Book 4 §63, 355–7. Schopenhauer makes a comparison between Kant's distinction between a phenomenal world and the things-in-themselves and the doctrine that all human cognition is illusory or behind a "veil of maya." See *The Thirteen Principal Upanishads,* trans. Robert Ernest Hume (Oxford: Oxford University Press, 1921): the doctrine of maya is in the Svetasvatara Upanishad 4.9–10, 404, cf. 38. Schopenhauer also argues that the transmigration of souls and ultimate promise of Nirvana is the popular version of the sages' philosophical view of the unity of all being beyond individual phenomenal experience. These views, and the ultimate possibility of fusing with "the All" are expressed in the Maitri Upanishad (esp. pp. 437 and 458).

15. Oswald Spengler, *The Decline of the West* (1917), an abridged version, trans. C. F. Atkinson (London: George, Allen and Unwin 1961). The original, *Der Untergang des Abendlandes: Umrisse einer Morphologie der Weltge- schichte,* is in two volumes (Munich: C. H. Beck). A useful brief summary of some of the ideas in the book can be found in Spengler's *Man and Technics* (London: European Book Society, 1992).

16. For a description of what Gadamer understands by "Neo-Kantianism," see his description of the thinking of Paul Natorp in *Philosophical Appren- ticeships,* 21–26.

17. See Chapter 1, note 1, p. 143.

18. *Dasein* means "existence" or "being-there." I have left it in German be- cause it is used in a technical sense by Heidegger, and occasionally by Gadamer himself, especially in his early work *Plato's Dialectical Ethics.* It is not synonymous with "consciousness" because whereas that term im- plies a distinct entity that tries to understand or assimilate a world around it (as in Descartes), Heidegger used the term "Dasein" to suggest that on the contrary we are always already part of, and involved in, the world.

19. Gadamer's discussion of "prejudice" as a precondition of all understand- ing, and of the possibility of overturning prejudices by means of a "fusion of horizons" can be found in *Truth and Method,* 271–307.

20. Augustine, *De Civitate Dei Contra Paganos* (417–426), 11.25 (para. C), trans. Gerald G. Walsh and Mother Grace Monahan in *Writings of Saint Augustine* Volume 7 (City of God) (Washington, D.C.: The Catholic University Press of America, 1952), 227: "I know that we ought to say that a person *enjoys* what he produces, but merely *makes use* of practice. The point of this distinction seems to be that a thing enjoyed (*frui*) is related directly to ourselves and not to something else, whereas a thing used (*uti*) is sought as a means to some other end."

21. Aristotle, *Metaphysics* 1.1.981b22–24.

22. This is supposedly established during the discussion in *Republic* 4.435–442.

23. For more on this, see *Reason in the Age of Science*, 74–5.

24. See *The Idea of the Good in Platonic-Aristotelian Philosophy*, especially Chapter 5.

25. I.e., Aristotle.

26. Aristotle, *Nichomachean Ethics*, 10.7.1177 a19-b26.

27. Aristotle, *Metaphysics*, 12.9.1074b15–34.

28. The reference here is to Aristotle's characterization of the imperishable human soul at *De Anima*, 1.4.408b25: *"Kai to noein de kai to theorein marainetai allou tinos eso phtheiromenou, auto de apathes estin."* "And thinking and contemplation (*to noein kai to theorein*) are only quenched by the death of some other thing that they are within, and are themselves unaffected." Gadamer takes this description of the soul to concern "witnessing" and "involvement"—his sense of "theoria"—rather than isolated consciousness. He may also be gesturing here toward a possible etymological connection between the Greek words "theoria" and *theos* (God).

29. The reference is to Aristotle's *Nichomachean Ethics* 10.7.1177a20, but this is not quite what Aristotle says, let alone something that he "stresses." He says: *"Kratiste te gar haute [theorein] estin he energeia."* "For it [contemplation] is the highest form of activity." But he has distinguished *theoria* as one of three kinds of *energeia*, the others being *poiesis* and *praxis*, and he does not relax his distinction between theory and practice in saying that theory is an activity.

3
The Power of Reason

1. "Practical or political science."

2. Aristotle, *Nichomachean Ethics*, 3.3.1112b12 and 32–33.

3. Gadamer uses two different words in this book that I have translated as

"rationality," and there is a stark contrast between them. *Vernünftigkeit* is the "reasonableness" that derives from Gadamer's notion of practical reason, while *Rationalität* (first used on the last page of this chapter) is the dominant "rationality" of modern society that Gadamer detects in the word "rationalization." I have marked each occurrence of "rationality" in my translation with its German original, except where it is obvious which sense is intended. More on Gadamer's conception of rationality can be found in his essay "Historical Transformations of Reason," but as that essay was originally published in English it does not explain the distinction between the two German words.

4. Christiaan Huygens, *Horologium Oscillatorium* (and *De Vi Centrifuga*). *The Pendulum Clock,* trans. Richard J. Blackwell (Ames: Iowa State University Press, 1986). Galileo Galilei, *Two New Sciences,* trans. Sillman Drake (University of Wisconsin Press, 1974).

5. René Descartes, *A Discourse on Method,* trans. John Veitch (London: J. M. Dent [Everyman], 1912).

6. Plato, *Gorgias,* 462d–465b and 500b–501b.

7. See Gadamer's essay on "The Limitations of the Expert" in *Applied Hermeneutics,* 181–192.

8. Poetry is, presumably, included in the parody of universal legislation at *Statesman,* 299d–e.

9. Heraclitus, Diels-Kranz fragment number 44, from Diogenes Laertius, *Lives of Eminent Philosophers,* 9.1.2: "Machesthai chre ton demon huper tou nomou [huper tou ginomenou] hokos huper teicheos." "It is necessary for the common people to fight for the law [for what has come about] in the same way as for the city wall." There is some evidence that *nomos* ("law") still had the interpretation Gadamer suggests for Heraclitus, although some scholars (e.g., M. Marcovich *Heraclitus* (Merida, Venezuela: Los Andes University Press, 1967), 94) take it to mean "law" as in the constitution of a city. The first, basic, meaning of the word offered in Liddell and Scott's *Lexicon* is "that which is in habitual practice, use or possession," and they quote Heraclitus fragment 114 ("all human laws are nourished by one law, the divine law") as an instance of *nomos* meaning "usage or custom." Charles Kahn offers a reading more compatible with Gadamer's in *The Art and Thought of Heraclitus* (Cambridge: Cambridge University Press, 1979), 117–118 and 179–181.

10. Quintus Aurelius Symmachus, *Relationes,* 3.10, in Otto Seeck (ed.) *Q. Aurelii Symmachi Quae Supersunt* (Berlin: Weidmann, 1883/1961), 282. Translation in R. H. Barrow (ed.) *Prefect and Emperor: The Relationes of*

Symmachus A.D. 384 with Translation and Notes (Oxford: Clarendon, 1973).

4
The Ideal of Practical Philosophy

1. Gadamer has paid a good deal of attention to the status of the *Geistes-wissenschaften*. See the beginning of *Truth and Method* (3–9) and the essays "Truth in the Human Sciences" and "Practical Philosophy as a Model of the Human Sciences."

2. John Stuart Mill, *A System of Logic, Ratiocinative and Inductive* (1872), *Collected Works* vols. 7–8 (London: Routledge and Kegan Paul, 1973–1974).

3. Sextus Empiricus, *Pros Dogmatikous* and *Pros Mathematikous*. Sextus actually questioned logic, physics, ethics, literary scholarship, rhetoric, geometry, arithmetic, astrology, and music. He was skeptical about all branches of learning, and had plenty to say about the "great domain of speaking and writing well" in the first book of *Pros Mathematikous,* which is called *Pros Grammatikous,* even if he does not specifically mention what we now call history.

4. Plutarch, *Lives of the Noble Grecians and Romans,* trans. Dryden (London: Encyclopaedia Brittanica, 1990).

5. Thucydides, *The History of the Peloponnesian War,* trans. Rex Warner (Harmondsworth: Penguin, 1954).

6. Moritz Schlick, "On the Foundation of Knowledge" (1934) in his *Philo-sophical Papers Volume II (1925–1936)* (Dordrecht: Reidel, 1979), 370–387. Schlick rejects a correspondence theory of truth in favor of a coherence theory, emphasizing that all scientific statements, including so-called "protocol-" or observation-statements, are hypotheses. As such, these statements cannot found science but instead play a role in the satisfaction of predictions, establishing the coherence of the scientific theory rather than the correspondence of scientific generalization to a Platonic "reality" external to science.

7. Max Weber, *The Methodology of the Social Sciences,* trans. A. Shils and Henry A. Finch (Glencoe, Ill.: The Free Press, 1949).

8. On hermeneutics, see Gadamer's essay "The Universality of the Herme-neutic Problem" in *Philosophical Hermeneutics,* 3–17, and also *Truth and Method,* 265–379.

9. Wilhelm Dilthey, *Der Aufbau der geschichtlichen Welt in den Geisteswissen-schaften,* in his *Gesammelte Schriften,* vol. 7 (Leipzig & Berlin: B. G.

Teubner, 1927), 146–152. Gadamer makes this claim about Dilthey's appropriation of Hegel's doctrine of objective Spirit in more detail in *Truth and Method*, 228–231.

10. See Dilthey, *Die Entstehung der Hermeneutik* (1900) and *Leben Schleiermachers* (1870), in his *Gesammelte Schriften*, vol. 5 (Leipzig & Berlin: B. G. Teubner, 1924) and vol. 13, (Göttingen: Vandenhoeck & Ruprecht, 1970), respectively.

11. Edmund Husserl, *The Crisis of European Sciences and Transcendental Phenomenology*, trans. David Carr (Evanston: Northwestern University Press, 1970), Part IIIA (1937).

12. In *Being and Time*. This actual phrase appears in that book in a footnote (490, I.3.note i) where Heidegger refers the reader back to his earlier lectures. An example of the concept in those lectures can be found in vol. 61 of his *Gesamtausgabe* (his 1921/2 lectures on Aristotle) (Frankfurt: Klostermann, 1985), 187–8.

13. Aristotle, *Metaphysics*, 6.1.1025b25: "hoste ei pasa dianoia e praktike e poietike e theoretike, he phusike theoretike tis a eie," "Insofar as all thinking is either practical, creative, or theoretical, natural science is theoretical." *Poiesis*, the Greek word from which "poetry" is derived, just means "making" or "doing."

14. Gadamer discusses this importance of human finitude in his criticism of Dilthey's position in *Truth and Method*, 231–236 and 357–358.

15. Aristotle, *Nichomachean Ethics*, 1.7.1098b2 ff. (Gadamer's own note).

16. See Chapter 1, note 20, p. 145.

17. Max Weber, "The Nature of Social Action" from *Economy and Society* (1910, first published posthumously in 1922). In *Max Weber: Selections in Translation* (Cambridge: Cambridge University Press, 1978), 28. Weber divides behavior into four kinds: rational means-end behavior, rational principled or value-promoting behavior, emotional behavior, and traditional behavior.

18. Aristotle, *Nichomachean Ethics* 1.1.1095a3 ff. (Gadamer's own note).

19. I have retained the abbreviated ending from the version of this essay in *Lob der Theorie*. The longer version, written for a book of essays on the work of Theodor Litt, concludes from this point as follows:

"Here Aristotelian thought takes a path of its own which, if I am right, is a good model for our own thinking about human knowledge and its historicity. To follow Aristotle is not to start from a general concept of science and then look at the various different kinds of human knowledge, but to chase the linguistic medium that transmits this knowledge and so to ground it in its true origin, the reality of human society. It is not just a matter of showing the central position of language and linguistic mediation in philosophical or, say, social scientific theory, but precisely also of making explicit the normative implications of the things that language mediates.

"This comes as no surprise. Dilthey's admirable enterprise of a Critique of Historical Reason was marked and, as we perceive today, also hindered by the model of experimental scientific method. His resistance to the neo-Kantian theory of value (Rickert) may well have been right, of course. But his mere opposition to it certainly had to be overcome, and this is what Theodor Litt tried to do. In 1941, when I had just become the youngest member of the Saxon Science Academy in Leipzig, I heard Litt give a lecture there on 'Universals in the Structure of Human-Scientific Knowledge' which seemed to me to compound the position he had already worked out in a lovely book in 1930, which was a synthesis between Kant and Herder. He said that language bridged the gap between universals and individual particulars, and this certainly came close to my own attempt to use Heidegger's ontological critique of Greek metaphysics and the modern subjectivity-based thinking that it engendered to improve the self-understanding of the human sciences. Today I still find some proximity to Litt, for example in his defense of everyday language against the construction of 'pure' concepts and terminology that is fully justified only in the natural sciences. Litt learned to articulate his own thinking in terms of Hegel's dialectic of universal and particular and the fusion of determinant and reflective judgment: this touched the hermeneutic nerve. I tried myself to go beyond the horizon of modern philosophy of science and the human sciences to display the hermeneutic problem in humanity's fundamental linguisticality. In the end phronesis, the Aristotelian virtue of rationality, is the basic hermeneutic virtue. I formed my own ideas on this model. Thus hermeneutics as the theory of application, i.e. of bringing the universal and the individual together—became, for me, a central philosophical task.

"Theodor Litt would probably oppose my attempts at thinking by saying that a philosophical justification of the human sciences on the model of Aristotelian phronesis would have to admit to positing an a priori that was more than just the result of empirical generalization. But it is always a misunderstanding to see the principle of Aristotle's practical philosophy as the 'that' without recognizing that as philosophy—and thus as a desire for theoretical knowledge—it couldn't itself depend on those elements of experience that it encounters as a concrete fulfillment of ethos or practically effected reason. Thus Litt would insist on the transcendental reflection that was also pursued by Husserl and even by the Heidegger of Being and Time. But even if this is better than an empiricist or inductivist theory, it seemed to me (and it still does) that it overlooks the fact that living practice provides this kind of reflection with the foundations and limits which it can sometimes rise above. This insight is not available to a reflection that takes the idealist step up to 'Spirit' (*Geist*). Thus in the end I still think it's right for one's thinking about the good in human life to set its own limits with the kind of Aristotelian caution that, perhaps with Plato, rightly forces philosophical ideas—which are certainly more than mere empirical generalizations—to remain tied to their own finitude and to finitude as we experience it in our own historical relativity."

Cf. Heinrich Rickert, *The Limits of Concept Formation in Natural Science* (1902), trans. Guy Oakes (Cambridge: Cambridge University Press, 1986), 215–236. Rickert argues that values are intrinsic to both human and natural sciences, but that the formal concept of value is itself objective, since, as it is fundamental to the will, it underlies all attempts to gain knowledge of any kind. On this basis he aims to go beyond Kant in promoting history to the same level of rigorous objectivity as natural science.

Theodor Litt, *Kant und Herder als Deuter der Geistigen Welt* (Leipzig, 1930).

Theodor Litt, *Das Allgemeine im Aufbau der geisteswissenschaftlichen Erkenntnis* (1941) (Hamburg: Meiner, 1980).

5
Science and the Public Sphere

1. The best source on Wilhelm von Humboldt in English, which also gives an excellent background to the history of the conception of *Bildung*, is Paul R. Sweet's two-volume work *Wilhelm von Humboldt: A Biography* (Columbus: Ohio State University Press, 1978 and 1980).
2. See Gadamer's "Notes on Planning for the Future" in *Applied Hermeneutics*, 165–180.
3. See Gadamer's discussion of "judgment" in *Truth and Method*, 30–34.
4. Gadamer explains his idea of experience, and his distinction between Erlebnis and Erfahrung in *Truth and Method*, 70 and 346–362.
5. Hegel, *The Phenomenology of Spirit* (1807), trans. A. V. Miller (Oxford: Clarendon, 1977), 118 "Work, on the other hand, is desire held in check, fleetingness staved off."
6. Charles Secondat, Baron de Montesquieu, *The Spirit of the Laws* (1748),

trans. Thomas Nugent (New York: Hafner, 1949), 9.6, 151. "When the legislative and executive powers are united in the same person, or in the same body of magistrates, there can be no liberty."

7. Plato, *Republic*, 7.520e-521b.

8. Aristotle, *Metaphysics*, 1.1.980a1.

9. Gadamer is presumably referring to *The Phenomenology of Spirit*, 298-299 (where Bildung is translated as "culture"), but it is not easy to recognize precisely this idea in Hegel's text.

10. Thales of Miletus was one of the "seven sages," and is indeed thought of as the first "philosopher." Diogenes Laertius, in the first chapter of his *Lives of Eminent Philosophers*, trans. R. D. Hicks (London: Heinemann [Loeb], 1950), however, tells this story rather differently: "It is said that once, when he was taken out of doors by an old woman in order that he might observe the stars, he fell into a ditch, and his cry for help drew from the old woman the retort, 'How can you expect to know all about the heavens, Thales, when you cannot even see what is just before your feet?'" 1.34.1-4.

6

Science as an Instrument of Enlightenment

1. Immanuel Kant, *What Is Enlightenment?*, trans. Lewis White Beck (University of Chicago Press, 1950), VIII, 35-41: "Enlightenment is man's release from his self-incurred tutelage. Tutelage is man's inability to make use of his understanding without direction from another. Self-incurred is this tutelage when its cause lies not in lack of reason but in lack of resolution and courage to use it without direction from another. *Sapere aude!* 'Have the courage to use your own reason!'—that is the motto of enlightenment." The phrase "sapere aude" itself is from Horace, *Ars poetica*.

2. Friedrich Nietzsche, *The Will to Power*, trans. Walter Kaufmann and R. J. Hollingdale (London: Weidenfeld and Nicolson, 1967), 94-95 ff. (posthumously published writings from the 1880s).

3. Jacob Burckhardt, *The Civilization of the Renaissance in Italy*, trans. S. G. C. Middlemore (London: Allen & Unwin, 1921). See also N. Nelson "Individualism as a Criterion of the Renaissance" *Journal of English and Germanic Philosophy* 32, 1933, 316-334.

4. René Descartes, *A Discourse on Method*, trans. John Veitch (London: J. M. Dent [Everyman], 1912).

5. Descartes, *Meditations on the First Philosophy*, published in the same book.

6. Descartes, *Discourse on Method,* V, 44–46.
7. Kant, *Critique of Judgement* (1790), part 2 "Critique of Teleological Judgement," trans. James Creed Meredith (Oxford: Clarendon, 1952).
8. See Kant, *Critique of Practical Reason and Other Writings in Moral Philosophy,* trans. Lewis White Beck (Chicago: University of Chicago Press, 1949).
9. Descartes never published a work on ethics, although some of his letters were gathered together with extracts from the third section of the *Passions of the Soul* after his death, and published under the title *Ethice in Methodum et Compendium* (London: W. Davies, 1685). These letters can now be found in *Descartes: His Moral Philosophy and Psychology,* ed. John J. Blom (Hassocks: Harvester, 1978). Gadamer's claim here can be assessed in the light of a few sentences from Blom's introduction, xvi–xviii:

   "Descartes assigned a perfected philosophy, and the moral autonomy it implies, only to God. . . . Moreover, Descartes knew that the responsible application of the sciences requires an understanding of the metaphysical structure and purpose of man—of the causes that lay hold on man, his powers of self-determination, the kinds of realities to which he can relate, and the solidity of the enjoyments he may take in them. . . . On [Descartes'] metaphysical picture hinged his more detailed discussion of 'virtue', which he defined as the correct reasoning that should guide our practice. On that same picture likewise depended his conception of the humane application of the sciences. . . . He also insisted that man's nervous system makes it more difficult for some to thwart their passions or even to acquire the knowledge needed for truly virtuous or voluntary action. He left no doubt that without a study of the body there could be no solid moral philosophy and psychology—no finished morale."

   Hence Descartes' ethics is provisional only in that it cannot be complete until we have a complete picture of the physical workings of the human body and the metaphysical status of man's free will: he certainly thought that his method could be applied to those questions, even if he believed that the complete picture itself (required for ethics) could be reached only by God.
10. Compare *Reason in the Age of Science,* 78–80, where Gadamer talks of the work of the critical theorists (such as Habermas) as "emancipatory reflection" and goes on to analyze the notion of "utopia."
11. Aristotle, *De Anima,* 3.8.432a1.
12. See Gadamer's writings on this topic in *The Enigma of Health.*

7

The Idea of Tolerance 1782–1982

1. *Der Hausball—eine deutsche National-Geschichte* was printed by Von Tratt-
nern in Vienna in 1781, and claimed only to be by "V***." It appears in
vol. 5 of *Goethes Werke*, ed. Friedrich Strehlke (Berlin: Gustav Hempel),
269–275, and was also reprinted in an extended version, without the introduction to which Gadamer refers, by Carl Konegen in Vienna in 1883.
The introduction runs like this (I include the German because the text is
so rare):

"Die neusten literarischen Nachrichten aus der Hauptstadt unseres
Vaterlandes versichern alle einmüthiglich, daß daselbst die Morgen-
röthe des schönsten Tages einzubrechen anfange, und ob wir gleich uns
ziemlich entfernt von jenen Gegenden befinden, so sind wir doch auch
geneigt, ebendasselbe zu glauben. Denn gewiß, es kann eine Schaar von
wilden Sonnenverehrern nicht mit einer größeren Inbrunst, mit einem
gewaltsameren Jauchzen und durch alle Glieder laufenden Entzücken die
Ankunft der Himmelstönigin begrüßen, als unsre Wiener, freilich auf
eine gleichfalls rohe Art, die ersten Strahlen einer gesegneten Regierung
Joseph des II. verehren. Wir wünschen ihm und ihnen den schönsten
Tag; die gegenwärtigen Augenblicke aber gleichen jenen Stunden des
Morgens, wo aus allen Tiefen und von allen Bächen aussteigende Nebel
die nächste Ankunft der Sonne verkündigen."

"The latest literary notices from the capital city of our Fatherland all
unanimously assert that the morning blush of the most beautiful day is
beginning to break there; and if we immediately find ourselves to be fairly
remote from those parts, we are still inclined also to believe the same
thing. For surely a sect of savage sun-worshippers could not welcome the
arrival of the goddess who tints the sky with a greater ardor, with a more
violent jubilation and rapture running through all its members, than [that
with which] our Vienna, admittedly in a similarly crude way, worships
the first rays of Joseph II's blessed reign. We wish him and his the most
beautiful day; but the present moments are like those hours of the morning that herald the next appearance of the sun from out of depths and
through all the fog that comes off the brooks."

2. The doctrine that the bread and wine used in Communion actually
become the body and the blood of Christ.

3. Benedict de Spinoza, *Tractatus Theologico-Politicus*, trans. Samuel Shirley
(Leiden: E. J. Brill, 1989).

4. Gotthold Ephraim Lessing, *Nathan der Weise* (1779), trans. E. K. Corbett as *Lessing's Nathan the Wise* (London: Kegan Paul, Trench & Co., 1883). This edition contains an introduction explaining the controversy. The play is set in Jerusalem at the time of the crusades, and its hero, Nathan, is a Jew. Nathan, Saladin, and a young Templar, whom Saladin has spared because he reminds him of his brother and who has then rescued Nathan's daughter from a fire, all express repeatedly the view that one can be truly good and pious only in overlooking the dogmatic details of one's own religion and treating everybody with love and understanding.

5. Hermann Lübbe, *Philosophie nach der Aufklärung* (Düsseldorf/Vienna: Econ, 1980), 214. Lübbe also makes a general point about the importance of the flow of trade in opposition to Gadamer's theory of understanding in his *Geschichtsbegriff und Geschichtsinteresse* (Basel/Stuttgart: Schwabe & Co, 1977), 227-230.

6. Johann Christoph Friedrich von Schiller, *Don Karlos:* the only recent translation I have found is by James Maxwell (Birmingham: Oberon Books, 1987). Carlos is the Spanish Infant (heir to the throne), and the woman he loves and to whom he was briefly betrothed has married his father, the King. Spain is currently putting down a revolt in Flanders, where Carlos, the new Queen, and their friend the Marquis of Posa all studied together and developed ideals of freedom. Posa endeavors to make the King see the value in sending Carlos to Flanders to quell the revolt without mass slaughter: the last scene of Act One is of particular relevance here.

7. The text of Mozart's *The Magic Flute* is by Emanuel Schikaneder, and there is a translation by Adrian Mitchell (London: Glen Freebairn and Associates, 1966). Sarastro is at first thought to be an evil tyrant who has kidnapped an innocent girl, but turns out to be a thoroughly wise and enlightened king, slandered by superstition and rumor, who rules over initiates who hold him in the highest regard. The words of his aria:

> In diesen heil'gen Hallen
> Kennt man die Rache nicht!
> Und ist ein Mensch gefallen
> Führt Liebe ihn zur Pflicht.
> Dann wandelt er an Freundes Hand
> Vergnügt und froh ins bessre Land.
> In diesen heil'gen Mauern
> Wo Mensch den Menschen liebt—
> Kann kein Verräter lauern

Weil man dem Freund vergibt.
Wen solche Lehren nicht erfreun,
Verdienet nicht ein Mensch zu sein.

Within these holy walls
Revenge is quite unknown!
When there's a man who falls
Love brings him to his own.
Then, glad and sated, hand in hand,
He strolls into a better land.
Within these holy walls
Where all by love must live—
Betrayal never calls
Because we all forgive.
And he who doesn't like this plan
Does not deserve to be a man.

8. Kant, *Religion Within the Limits of Reason Alone* (1793), trans. Theodore M. Greene and Hoyt H. Hudson (La Salle: Open Court, 1934 and 1960).

9. For Gadamer's notion of *Wirkungsgeschichte* ("effective history" or "the history of influence") see *Truth and Method,* 300–307.

10. "Who owns the territory dictates the religion."

11. For the importance Gadamer accords to conversation, and especially to "proper conversation" (*eigentliche Gespräch*), see *Truth and Method,* 358–369.

12. Claude-Henri de Rouvroy, Comte de Saint-Simon: see *The Political Thought of Saint-Simon,* trans. and ed., Ghita Ionescu (Oxford: Oxford University Press, 1976).

13. Gadamer also urges the need to promote solidarity in *Reason in the Age of Science,* 85–87.

14. Nietzsche, *The Will to Power.*

15. Max Weber, *Parlament und Regierung im neugeordneten Deutschland* (1918), in his *Gesammelte politische Schriften* (Tübingen: J. C. B. Mohr (Paul Siebeck), 1958) 3rd edition, 1971, 330–333.

16. See page 108.

17. Especially in Socrates' speeches from 50a onward.

18. Max Weber, *Politik als Beruf* (1919), in his *Gesammelte politische Schriften,* 3rd edition, (Tübingen: J. C. B. Mohr [Paul Siebeck], 1971), 546–551.

19. In act 3 scene 7, Nathan wins the respect of Saladin by telling him the following story. A man has a magical ring that makes people love him, and

leaves it in his will to his best-loved son, ordaining that it should always be passed on to the son its bearer loves best. Generations later, the owner of the ring has three sons he loves equally and promises it individually to each of them. Unwilling to break his promises he has two copies made: after his death the sons wrangle over which was the real ring. They appeal to a judge who points out the rings are a sign of their father's equal love for all of them, that it is impossible to tell the real one except by which ring-bearer is most loved (the supposed result of its magical power), and that they should therefore each believe their own ring to be the true one and love the other two. This is explicitly interpreted as an analogy for God's giving Christianity, Judaism, and Islam to man.

8
Isolation as a Symptom of Self-Alienation

1. The whole book of Job concerns anger against God and humanity. Christ's agony is related in Matthew 26.30–46, Mark 14.26–42, and Luke 22.39–46.
2. Matthew 27.46: "And about the ninth hour Jesus cried with a loud voice, saying, Eli, Eli, lama sabachthani? that is to say, My God, my God, why hast thou forsaken me?" Also at Mark 15.34.
3. Euripides, *Helen*, 560 *HELENE: o theoi! theos gar kai to gignoskein philous.* HELEN (on recognizing Menelaus): O gods! For god is the recognizing of friends.
4. Friedrich Hölderlin, *On Religion* (c. 1797), trans. Thomas Pfau in his edition of Hölderlin's *Essays and Letters on Theory* (Albany: State University of New York Press, 1988), 92–93: "And hence everyone would have his own god to the extent that everyone has his own sphere in which he works and which he experiences, and only to the extent that several men have a common sphere in which they work and suffer humanely, that is, elevated above basic needs, only to that extent do they have a common divinity; and if there exists a sphere in which they all exist simultaneously and to which they bear a relation of more than basic needs, then, and only to that extent do they all have a common divinity."
5. Johann Wolfgang von Goethe, *Wilhelm Meisters Lehrjarhe,* 2.13, in Goethe's *Werken,* vol. 7 (Munich: C. H. Beck, 1950–1968), 137. Translation by H. M. Waidson available as "Wilhelm Meister's Years of Apprenticeship" (London: J. Calder, 1977–1979), 120–121. The whole song:

> Wer sich der Einsamkeit ergibt,
> Ach! der ist bald allein;

Ein jeder lebt, ein jeder liebt,
Und läßt ihn seiner Pein.

Ja! laßt mich meiner Qual!
Und kann ich nur einmal
Recht einsam sein,
Dann bin ich nicht allein.

Es schlecht ein Liebender lauschend sacht,
Ob seine Freundin allein?
So überschleicht bei Tag und Nacht
Mich Einsamen die Pein,
Mich Einsamen die Qual.
Ach werd' ich erst einmal
Einsam im Grabe sein,
Da läßt sie mich allein!

Who devotes himself to solitude
Alas, is soon alone;
Other people live and love,
And leave him with his pain.

Yes, leave me my suffering!
If I can only once again
Find real solitude,
Then I am not alone.

A lover always burns to know
If his lover is on her own.
Thus over me by night and day creeps
The solitude of pain,
The solitude of suffering.
But once I can be
Alone in my grave,
Then it will leave me alone!

6. Nietzsche, *Thus Spoke Zarathustra*, trans. R. J. Hollingdale (Harmondsworth: Penguin, 1961).
7. Schiller, *On the Aesthetic Education of Man: in a series of letters* (Oxford: Clarendon, 1967). Especially letters 1–5.

8. Marx, *Capital* (1867), trans. Samuel Moore and Dr. Aveling, ed. Friedrich Engels (Moscow: Foreign Languages Publishing House, 1954) (6 volumes).

9. See Gadamer's essay on "Culture and Media."

10. Kant, *The Metaphysics of Morals* (1797) 2.2.2.47, 472, trans. Mary Gregor (Cambridge: Cambridge University Press, 1991). The reference is to this passage where Kant quotes Juvenal's phrase from Satires 2.6.165:

"The necessary combination of qualities is seldom found in one person (*rara avis in terris, nigroque simmilima cygno*), especially since the closest friendship requires that a judicious and trusted friend be also bound not to share the secrets entrusted to him with anyone else, no matter how reliable he thinks him, without explicit permission to do so.

"This (merely moral friendship) is not just an ideal but (like black swans) actually exists here and there in its perfection. . . ."

11. Aristotle, *Nichomachean Ethics,* 8 and 9.

12. One of the earliest written occurrences of this maxim is in Plato's *Phaedrus,* 279c5.

13. Plato, *Republic,* 4, especially 434e.

14. Hegel, *Lectures on the History of Philosophy* (1840), trans. E. S. Haldane (London: Kegan Paul, Trench, Trübner and Co Ltd, 1892), vol. 1, 152: "Philosophy is being at home with self, just like the homeliness of the Greek; it is man's being at home in his mind, at home with himself." The phrase Gadamer actually uses (*Sich-Einhausen*) does not appear in Hegel.

15. Hegel, *The Phenomenology of Spirit,* chapter 3.

9
Man and His Hand in Modern Civilization

1. Gadamer may have in mind section 14 of Nietzsche's *The Antichrist,* where Nietzsche talks of man losing the instinctive certainty of animals. See the translation by H. L. Mencken (Costa Mesa, California, 1980), 59.

2. Arnold Gehlen, *Zur Systematik der Anthropologie* (1942), part 5. See his *Gesamtausgabe,* vol. 4, 85–87 (Frankfurt am Main: Vittorio Klostermann, 1983).

3. Aristotle, *De Anima,* 3.8.432a1.

4. See Chapter 8, note 7.

1. See especially *Philosophical Hermeneutics,* 20–26 and *Reason in the Age of Science,* 118–137.

2. Philip Melanchthon, *Elementorum Rhetorices,* which, although originally published in three books (1519), appears in its later two-book version (1531) in the collection of the writings of the Reformation thinkers edited by Carolus Gottlieb Bretschneider under the title *Corpus Reformatum.* It is found in vol. 13, *Philippi Melanthonis Opera Quae Supersunt Omnia Volumen XIII* (Halis Saxonum: Schwetschke & Son, 1846), 416–506.

3. Plato, *Gorgias,* 462d–465b and 500b–501b and *Phaedrus,* 268a–269c. The *Phaedrus* passage implies that rhetoric, in the sense of a knowledge of how to construct well-balanced speeches, is a necessary pre-requisite for dialectical inquiry into the truth, but it remains wholly disparaging of the claim that rhetoric might of itself be able to reach or display interesting truths of any kind.

4. Gadamer explains his understanding of "dialectic," and the distinction between Plato's notion and Hegel's (he never refers to Marx's or Sartre's), in *Dialogue and Dialectic* and *Hegel's Dialectic.* See also Chapter 7, note 11.

5. Gadamer uses the notion of "good-will" in his reply to Derrida: "Good-Will to Power" in *Dialogue and Deconstruction* (see bibliography under "Text and Interpretation").

6. In his lost treatise *On Imitation,* the substance of which is recounted in his *Letter to Gnaeus Pompeius,* 3–5. See Dionysius of Halicarnassus, *The Critical Essays,* vol. 2, trans. Stephen Usher (London: William Heinemann [Loeb], 1985) 370–399.

7. Kant, *Critique of Pure Reason* (1781 and 1787), trans. Norman Kemp Smith (Basingstoke: Macmillan, 1929), 41 (B1).

8. Gadamer discusses *sensus communis* in *Truth and Method,* 19–30.

9. The classic example would be Sigmund Freud, *The Interpretation of Dreams* (1900), trans. A. A. Brill (London: George Allen & Unwin Ltd, 1913).

10. Theodor Mommsen, *The History of Rome,* trans. William P. Dickson (London: Bentley, 1962–1966).

11. Translations of Lessing's comedies are comparatively rare. One relevant example (*Der Freigeist*) is translated as "The Freethinker" in *Three Comedies,* trans. Rev. J. J. Holroyd (Colchester: W. Totham, 1838).

12. As opposed to *"ungelehrt,"* which means "illiterate."

13. Walter Benjamin, *Ursprung des deutschen Trauenspiels* (1925) in his *Gesammelte Schriften*, 1.1 (Frankfurt-am-Main: Suhrkamp, 1974). Translated by John Osborne as *The Origin of German Tragic Drama* (London: NLB, 1977).

14. Perhaps Gadamer is not being entirely serious here, because at *Laws* 7.811c–d, Plato recommends legislation to the effect that all poetry and writing to be permitted in the state should emulate the style (and content) of his own dialogues. He has no recommendations about specific ways of using words to create a desired effect, beyond stipulations concerning the moral messages they may convey.

15. Probably Hans Detlef Jensen, author of *Altarmenische Chrestomathie* (1964) and *Die Schrift in Vergangenheit und Gegenwart* (1935).

16. *Hegel's Dialectic*, 41–43.

17. The 250th anniversary of his birth.

11
Good German

1. The name of the standard German dictionary.

2. In 1979, the Georg-Büchner-Preis (awarded by the German Academy for Language and Poetry) was won by Ernst Meister, a friend of Gadamer's who died that year, for his selected poems *Ausgewählte Gedichte 1932–1979* (Darmstadt: Luchterhand, 1979). The line Gadamer quotes, "listigen Töchter, die vogelgestimmten," does not, however, appear in that volume. Gadamer has written three pieces about Meister's poetry: "Ernst Meister, Gedenken V" (1977), "Gedicht und Gespräch: Überlegungen zu einer Textprobe Ernst Meisters" (1988), and "Denken im Gedicht" (1990). None of these has been translated into English, but they are all available in vol. 9 of Gadamer's *Gesammelte Werke* (Tübingen: JCB Mohr [Paul Siebeck], 1993).

3. Comte de Buffon: "Ces choses sont hors de l'homme, le style est l'homme même." *Discours sur le Style* (an address given to the Académie française on 25 August 1753).

4. Schopenhauer, *The World as Will and Representation* vol. 2, 122–126.

5. See Friedrich Gundolf's *Beiträge zur Literatur- und Geistesgeschichte* (Heidelberg: Lambert Schneider, 1980) or his book on *Goethe* (Berlin: Bondi, 1914).

6. The theater reviews of Paul Rilla have been published in book form under the title *Theaterkritiken* (Berlin: Henschelverlag, 1978).

7. Hugo von Hofmannsthal, a playwright especially noted for his German

versions of Greek tragedies, Stefan George, poet, Rainer Maria Rilke, author of the *Duino Elegies* and the *Sonnets to Orpheus*, and Friedrich Hölderlin, prolific poet and author of *Hyperion*.

8. The best example is the first sentence of Hölderlin's essay *On the Operations of the Poetic Spirit* (1800), trans. Thomas Pfau in his edition of Hölderlin's *Essays and Letters on Theory* (Albany: State University of New York Press, 1988), 62–64. The sentence begins "Once the poet is in control of the spirit," and two pages later it ends, "once he has realized all this, then he is only concerned with the receptivity of the subject matter to the ideal content and the ideal form."

9. See, for example, Max Kommerell, *Der Dichter als Führer in der deutschen Klassik* (1928) (Frankfurt-am-Main: Vittorio Klostermann, 1942).

10. See Karl Reinhardt, *Sophocles* (1953), trans. Hazel Harvey and David Harvey (Oxford: Blackwell, 1979).

11. See Dolf Sternberger, *Panorama of the Nineteenth Century* (1938), trans. Joachim Neugroschel (Oxford: Blackwell, 1977).

12. Publius Ovidius Naso, *Metamorphoses* 10.252: "ars adeo latet arte sua."

Glossary

Apodeixis	Greek	Conclusive proof.
Aporia	Greek	A puzzle or being at a loss. Plato's early dialogues end in aporia when it is realized that no conclusion can be reached.
Aufheben	German	To cancel out and so to raise to a higher level (Hegel). In more normal usage, to get beyond something.
Bildung	German	Cultivation, up-bringing, culture, edification (Rorty). Bilden means to form.
Contemplatio	Latin	Contemplation, Gadamer's Latin translation of the Greek theoria.
Dasein	German	Existence, being-there (Heidegger).
Delun	Greek	Revealing (what something is).
Energeia	Greek	Activity.
Eudaimonia	Greek	Happiness.
Eumenia	Greek	Good-will.
Gegenstand	German	Object. German also uses the word Objekt.
Geisteswissenschaften	German	The human sciences. Roughly equivalent to what we would call the humanities and social sciences.

Hermeneutics		Interpretation theory. The idea that an individual's understanding is central to all knowledge.
Kalon	Greek	Beautiful.
Kata syntheken	Greek	By convention.
Koine sympheron	Greek	Useful in common to all.
Lebenswelt	German	Life-world (Husserl).
Leidensdruck	German	Pressure of suffering.
Logos	Greek	Conventionally translated "reason." Gadamer emphasizes its etymological connection with word and language.
Mathemata	Greek	Things that are learned.
Mythos	Greek	Myth, legend.
Neugier	German	Curiosity. Literally, greed for novelty.
Nomos	Greek	Law.
Paideia	Greek	Education, up-bringing.
Philia	Greek	Friendship.
Phronesis	Greek	Practical wisdom.
Poiesis	Greek	Making, construction: composition of poetry.
Praxis	Greek & German	Practice.
Prohairesis	Greek	Choice.
Protreptic		Writings that promote the theoretical examination of life.
Rational obligation (rationale Sachzwang)		The inevitability of events that are determined by rationalization.
Sapere aude	Latin	Dare to know.
Sensus communis	Latin	Sense of community, communal good sense.

Speculatio	Latin	Speculation, reflection. Gadamer emphasizes its etymological derivation from speculum, a mirror.
Syntheke	Greek	Convention.
Theoria	Greek	Theory, contemplation, witnessing.
Vernünftigkeit	German	Rationality, but in the sense of reasonableness, being sensible, as opposed to rationalizing.
Wissenschaft	German	Science.

Bibliography

Gadamer in English

The following is a selective rather than a comprehensive list. See Etsuro Makita's *Gadamer—Bibliographie*. Frankfurt: Peter Lang, 1994.

Applied Hermeneutics (Hans-Georg Gadamer on Poetry, Education and History). Eds. D. Misgeld and G. Nicholson. Albany: State University of New York Press, 1992.

"Concerning Empty and Ful-filled Time." *The Southern Journal of Philosophy* 8 (4) 341–354, 1970.

"The Conflict of Interpretations." In R. Bruzina and B. Wiltshire (eds.). *Phenomenology: Dialogues and Bridges.* Albany: State University of New York Press, 1982.

"The Continuity of History and the Existential Moment." *Philosophy Today* 16 (3/4) 230–240, 1972.

"Culture and Media." In A. Honneth (ed). *Cultural-Political Interventions in the Unfinished Project of Enlightenment.* Cambridge, Mass.: MIT Press, 1992.

Dialogue and Dialectic. New Haven: Yale University Press, 1980.

The Enigma of Health. Cambridge: Polity Press, 1995.

Hegel's Dialectic. New Haven: Yale University Press, 1976.

Heidegger's Ways. Albany: State University of New York Press, 1994.

"Hermeneutics and Social Science." *Cultural Hermeneutics* 2 (2) 307–366, 1975.

"The Hermeneutics of Suspicion." In G. Shapiro and A. Sica (eds.). *Hermeneutics: Questions and Prospects.* Amherst: University of Massachusetts Press, 1984.

"Historical Transformations of Reason." In T. Geraets (ed.). *Proceedings of the International Symposium on Rationality Today.* Ottawa: University of Ottawa Press, 1979.

"The History of Concepts and the Language of Philosophy." *International Studies in Philosophy* 18 (3) 1–16, 1986.

The Idea of the Good in Platonic-Aristotelian Philosophy. New Haven: Yale University Press, 1986.

Literature and Philosophy in Dialogue. Albany: State University of New York Press, 1994.

"Natural Science and Hermeneutics: The Concept of Nature in Ancient Philosophy." In J. Cleary (ed.). *Proceedings of the Boston Area Colloquium in Ancient Philosophy,* vol. 1. Lanham: University Press of America, 1986.

"On the Possibility of a Philosophical Ethics." In R. Beiner and W. Booth (eds.). *Kant and Political Philosophy: The Contemporary Legacy.* New Haven: Yale University Press, 1993.

Philosophical Apprenticeships. Cambridge, Mass.: MIT Press, 1985.

Philosophical Hermeneutics. Berkeley: University of California Press, 1976.

Plato's Dialectical Ethics. New Haven: Yale University Press, 1991.

"Practical Philosophy as a Model of the Human Sciences." *Research in Phenomenology* (9) 74–85, 1980.

"The Problem of Historical Consciousness." In P. Rabinow and W. Sullivan (eds.). *Interpretive Social Science: A Reader.* Berkeley: University of California Press, 1979.

Reason in the Age of Science. Cambridge, Mass.: MIT Press, 1981.

The Relevance of the Beautiful and Other Essays. Cambridge: Cambridge University Press, 1986.

"Text and Interpretation." In D. Michelfelder and R. Palmer (eds.). *Dialogue and Deconstruction: the Gadamer-Derrida Encounter.* Albany: State University of New York Press, 1989.

Truth and Method (2nd edition with revised translation). London: Sheed and Ward, 1989.

"Truth in the Human Sciences." In B. R. Wachterhauser (ed.). *Hermeneutics and Truth.* Evanston, Ill.: Northwestern University Press, 1994.

"What Is Truth?" In Wachterhauser (ed). *Hermeneutics and Truth.* Evanston, Ill.: Northwestern University Press, 1994.

Further Reading

Bernstein, Richard J. *Beyond Objectivism and Relativism: Science, Hermeneutics and Praxis.* Oxford: Blackwell, 1983.

———. *Philosophical Profiles: Essays in a Pragmatic Mode.* Philadelphia: University of Pennsylvania Press, 1986.

Caputo, John D. *Radical Hermeneutics: Repetition, Deconstruction and the*

Hermeneutic Project. Bloomington/Indianapolis: Indiana University
    Press, 1987.

Foster, Michael. *Gadamer and Practical Philosophy.* Atlanta: Scholars
    Press, 1991.

Grondin, Jean. *Introduction to Philosophical Hermeneutics.* New Haven:
    Yale University Press, 1995.

Hekman, Susan. *Hermeneutics and the Sociology of Knowledge.* Notre
    Dame, Ind.: University of Notre Dame Press, 1986.

Hollinger, Robert (ed.). *Hermeneutics and Praxis.* Notre Dame, Ind.:
    University of Notre Dame Press, 1985.

Ricoeur, Paul. *Hermeneutics and the Human Sciences.* Cambridge: Cam-
    bridge University Press, 1981.

Silverman, Hugh J. (ed.). *Gadamer and Hermeneutics: Science, Culture,
    Literature.* London: Routledge, 1991.

Simpson, Evan (ed.). *Anti-Foundationalism and Practical Reasoning.*
    Edmonton: Academic Publishing and Printing, 1987.

Smith, P. Christopher. *Hermeneutics and Human Finitude: Towards a
    Theory of Ethical Understanding.* New York: Fordham University Press,
    1991.

Sullivan, Robert R. *Political Hermeneutics: The Early Thinking of Hans-
    Georg Gadamer.* University Park: Pennsylvania State University Press,
    1989.

Vattimo, Gianni. *The End of Modernity: Nihilism and Hermeneutics in
    Post-Modern Culture.* Cambridge: Polity Press, 1988.

Wachterhauser, Brice R. (ed.). *Hermeneutics and Modern Philosophy.*
    Albany: State University of New York Press, 1986.

———. *Hermeneutics and Truth.* Evanston: Northwestern University
    Press, 1994.

Warnke, Georgia. *Gadamer: Hermeneutics, Tradition and Reason.* Cam-
    bridge: Polity Press, 1987.

Weinsheimer, Joel C. *Philosophical Hermeneutics and Literary Theory.* New
    Haven: Yale University Press, 1991.

Wright, Kathleen (ed.). *Festivals of Interpretation: Essays on Hans-Georg
    Gadamer's Work.* Albany: State University of New York Press, 1990.

Index

Culture (continued)
step in choosing, 8; in society,
15, 50, 90; distinctive of human
spirit, 34, 54, 114
Curiosity, 12, 21, 32
Cybernetics, 80–81

Dasein, xiii, 20, 30, 35, 55, 58
Davidson, Donald, xvi
Death, 11, 15, 34
Democracy, 63, 74, 95, 108, 122
Denotation, 127–128, 133
Derrida, Jacques, xv
Descartes, René, xv, 41, 77–78
Desires, 33
Dialectic, xxvi, 67, 112–113, 124,
131, 153
Dialogue, 56, 130. *See also* Conversation
Dilthey, Wilhelm, 54, 153
Dionysius of Halicarnassus, 125
Distance from self: brought by
language, xxix, 6, 10; basis of
theory, 20, 67; in Plato's guardians, 67; necessary for research,
68; required for cultivation, 120;
in writing, 131, 140
Distribution of goods, 32
Dogmatism, xxxiii, 49, 58
Domination of nature: effect on
world, vii, 88; result of modern
research, viii, 41, 55–56, 127;
technology as, xxxiv, 76–77;
effect on individual, 117
Drives, human, 34, 37

Ebner, Ferdinand, 4, 6
Ecology, xxxiv, 80
Economics, 37, 90, 95, 108

Education: aims of, 9, 69, 119,
120; classical heritage, 16, 18,
40; and the state, 63; value of
traditional, 136, 140–141
Egypt, ancient, 17, 33
Emancipatory utopia, viii, xxxiv,
79–80
Embodiment, xi
Ends, 68
Enlightenment: new one needed,
viii, xxxiv, 83; pride in reason, 1,
24, 37; response to religion, 3,
85; free-thinking, 62, 71, 86; history of, 71–83, 84, 86, 92; of the
twentieth century, 74, 89–90, 135
Epistemology, 27, 53
Equilibrium: instinctive and intellectual, xxxv, 116–117; political,
28, 67; arising from rational
obligation, 43; maintaining, 81;
upset by rationalization, 117. *See
also* Balance; Compromise
Ethics: *ethos*, xiv, 8, 58, 153; communal and practical, 7, 58, 59;
Kantian, 60, 79; non-empirical,
60, 153
Euclid, 128
Eudaimonia, 41. *See also* Good;
Happiness
Euripides, 102
Evolution, 115
Examples, 135
Existence, vii
Experience: empirical science,
39, 72, 126; of life, 53, 66, 110;
cannot found ethics, 153
Experts: social reliance on, viii,
xxxvi, 43–44, 75, 95; panel not
to be completed by philoso-

phers, 48; symbol of theory unrestrained by practical rationality, 57; researchers as, 62

Fact, xxvii, 31, 53, 54, 58
Facticity, xiii, 55. *See also* Finitude
Faith, 14-15, 37, 85, 89
Feedback, 80-81
Festival, xxv
Fichte, Johann Gottlieb, 139
Final Causes, 76
Finitude: key term, xxvii; complete understanding impossible, 12, 55, 81, 153; revealed in reconciliation, 14; recognition of allows practical rationality, 48, 58; overlooked by Dilthey, 55
Flexibility, 82
Force, 133
Forgiveness, 14
Formalism, 60
Forms, Platonic, xii, xxv
Forsaking, 102
Foucault, Michel, xv
Foundation, 154
Frankfurt-am-Main, Germany, xxi
Freedom: key term, xxxv; organized free time, 10; political, 37, 80, 86; for play in art and science, 68, 106, 116, 136, 140; definitions of, 79, 112, 122; bourgeois, in the Enlightenment, 86; as arbitrariness, is an illusion, 91; individuals' universal lack of in rationalized society, 96, 107, 109, 117; of speech, 97-98
Frege, Gottlob, xv
Freiburg, Germany, xx
French Revolution, 74, 87

Freud, Sigmund, 128-129, 142
Friedrich II, king of Prussia, 84, 97
Friendship, 102, 110-113 *passim*
Function, individual's in rationalized system, xxxiv, 95, 96, 99, 106, 117
Funding for research, xxxiv, 26, 65
Fusion of horizons, xvi, xxiv

Gadamer, Hans-Georg: philosophical project, vii; technique, xvi-xvii, xxxi, xxxvii; biography and anecdotes, xix-xxii, 85, 130, 133, 140-142; on Plato, xxv-xxvii; on hermeneutic understanding, xxviii; and Theodor Litt, 153
— *Truth and Method*: on incarnation, xi; described, xvii, xxi, xxiii; on method, xxii, xxxiv; on conversation, xxiv, xxx; on theory, xxv; summarized, xxvii; on language, xxix, xxxvi
— other works: *Plato's Dialectical Ethics*, xvii, xx; *Philosophical Apprenticeships*, xix; *Hegel's Dialectic*, xxi; *Praise of Theory*, xxii; *Reason in the Age of Science*, xxiii; *The Relevance of the Beautiful*, xxiv, xxv
Galileo, 23, 41, 51, 76, 127
Gehlen, Arnold, 115
Geisteswissenschaften. See Human Sciences
Generations, 91, 109
George, Stefan, xx, 96, 141
Gesture, 14
Goals, 59
God: creation, 3; and man, 11, 34,

God (continued)
102; defined, 20, 35, 102; object
of contemplation, 21–22; polytheistic, 21, 105; and science, 23,
39; in the Enlightenment, 23,
76, 78; the Trinity, 85. *See also*
Christianity; Religion
Goethe, Johann Wolfgang von,
xxi, 25, 27, 84, 103, 142
Good, the, xxvi, 7, 17–18, 19, 34,
154
Goods, 6, 32
Good-will, 124
Gorgias, 73
Grammar, 135
Greeks, ancient: developed science, 12, 33, 37, 50, 71, 101; custom of eulogy, 16; importance of
friendship, 110; Humanist view
of, 125; Heidegger's critique of,
153
Gundolf, Friedrich, 140

Habermas, Jürgen, xv, xvi, xxi,
xxix, xxxiv
Hamann, Richard, xx
Hand, the, 80, 116, 118
Happiness, 20, 34
Hartmann, Nicolai, xx
Health, 26, 30
Hegel, Georg Wilhelm Friedrich: master and servant, xxxv,
112–113; synthesis of spirit, 25;
influence, 54, 153; on work, 66;
on *Bildung*, 68; being at home
with oneself, 112; concept of
force, 133; writing style, 139;
mentioned, xv
Heidegger, Martin: hermeneutics
of facticity, xi, xxviii, 55; taught

Gadamer, xx; writing style, 139,
142; critique of subjectivity-
based thinking, 153; *Being and
Time*, 154; mentioned, xv
Heidelberg, Germany, xxii, 103
Heraclitus, 17, 48
Herder, Johann Gottfried, 2, 3, 24,
133
Hermeneutics: of facticity, xi, 55;
Gadamer's model, xxiii, 61, 153;
defined, xxviii; and concept of
fact, 31, 53; reconstruction of
meaning, 123
Hesiod, 71
Hesse, Hermann, 141
Historicism, xxvii
Historicity, 152*n*19. *See also* Fac-
ticity; Finitude
History, xviii, xxvii, 39, 52, 54, 56,
125, 154
Hitler, Adolf, xxi
Hofmannsthal, Hugo von, 141
Hölderlin, Friedrich, 3, 102, 141,
142
Homer, 22, 71
Human. *See* Mankind
Humaniora, 51, 54–55, 129
Humanism, 11, 25, 125
Human sciences: not methodi-
cal, viii, xxxiii, 56, 133; self-
understanding of, 50, 153; as
"moral sciences," 51, 60; episte-
mology of, 53
Humboldt, Wilhelm von, 62
Hume, David, 39
Husserl, Edmund, xx, 55, 128, 154
Huygens, Christiaan, 41

Idealism, 24–25, 27, 37, 154
Ideology critique, 27

Patriarchalism, 94

Philosophy: different kinds of, xv, 20, 57, 103; scope and methodology, xviii, 37, 48, 57, 101, 154; history of, xxxii, 12, 16, 20, 27, 103; writing style of German philosophers, 139; and poetry, 141

Phronesis. See Rationality, practical

Planets, 12

Planning, 43, 64, 93–94

Plato: Gadamer's reading, xii, xxiii, xxv-xxvii; and poetry, 1, 132; *Republic*, 8, 18, 19, 33, 40, 67, 69, 111; participation in political life, 16, 17, 19, 96; on rhetoric, 43, 44, 124; on astronomy and mathematics, 72; philosophy based in finitude, 154; mentioned, xv, xix

Play, 116, 117, 136, 137

Pleasure, 26

Pliny the Elder, 22

Plutarch, 52

Poetry, xiii, 13, 57, 134, 136, 137, 141

Politeness, 98

Politics: limiting abuse of power, 9, 66–67; in ancient Athens, 16; and theory, 18, 19, 67; responsibility of representatives, 37, 57; not scientific, 51, 56–57, 65; not in control of "the system," 92; utopia of rationalization, 93-94

Positivism, 37, 53

Power: evil of, 31, 93, 100; of reason, 37–38, 48; dialectic of, 67, 94; being powerful, 69, 104, 122; of calculation, 118

Practice: and theory, xxxii, xxxiv, 17, 19, 24, 36, 56, 66; and science,

42; professional training, 120; as transcendental foundation, 154

Praise, 16

Preaching, 125

Prejudices: questioning, xviii, xxix, 31, 71; in the Enlightenment, 45; technological dream and emancipatory utopia, 79–80; and instinctive senses, 118-119

Printing, 125

Privacy, 21, 109, 110

Profession, 19, 26, 105-106, 107, 120

Progress, 25–28 *passim*

Prohairesis, 8, 34, 57. *See also* Choice

Promise, 14

Prose, 125, 130-132, 138, 141–142

Protagoras, 73

Protestant Reformation, 86, 99, 125

Protreptic, xxii-xxiii, xxvi, 16

Psychoanalysis, 27, 107

Public opinion, 45

Purpose, freedom from, 19, 63, 68

Pythagoras, 50-51, 71, 111

Question, 12

Rationality.
—Economic (*Rationalität*), 48, 93, 98, 114, 119
—Means/end, 40, 59
—Practical (*Vernünftigkeit, Phronesis*): communal foundation of ethics, xiii, xxxiii, 40, 58–59; and finitude, xiii, 48; and taste, xiii; in Kant, 24, 87; basic hermeneutic virtue, 50, 153; and theory, 57, 60

Rationalization: of our existence
is impossible, vii; removes solidarity and freedom, xxxiv, 99,
107, 117; not an end in itself,
36; effect on research, 62–63; as
totalitarianism, 92, 93
Rational obligation (*Rationale
Sachzwang*), xxxv, 42–43, 46–47,
107–108
Reading, 123, 125
Reality, 30, 110
Reason: incarnate in existence,
vii; defined, xxxiii, 46, 119; and
logos, 4; and faith, 23, 76, 85;
practical, 24, 50, 87; social, 37–
49, 83; divided into pure theory
and practical rationality, 57–58
Recognition, 10
Reconciliation, 14
Reference, 13
Reformation, 86, 99, 125
Regulatory feedback, 80–81
Reinhardt, Karl, 142
Relativism, xxvii, 154
Religion: dialogue between faiths,
11, 89; as human interaction,
14–15, 88, 97; enlightenment
as critique of, 71; rational, 87;
solitude of prayer, 104. *See also*
Christianity; God
Rembrandt, 103
Renaissance, 75
Repetition compulsion, 107
Replaceability, 107
Reproduction, 2–3, 11
Research: accidental discoveries,
xxxi, 64; funding, xxxiv, 26; need
for, 12, 39; history of concept,
23, 130; pure and applied, 26,
63; in anthropology, 33; and

rhetoric, 45, 130; and experts,
62; freedom from purpose, 68–
69; easily misunderstood, 70;
conflict with ethics, 78; and
writing, 140. *See also* Science
Responsibility: of researchers, 46;
political, of the individual, 57–
58, 82–83, 108–109, 122; foundation of ethics, 79; for social
compulsions, 109; professional,
113
Rhetoric: used by Gadamer, xvi–
xvii; as communal world-view,
xxxvi, 52, 126, 128; Plato on, 43,
44, 124; of mass media, 44, 136;
aligned with politics and poetry,
57; and Enlightenment, 73;
move from speaking to writing,
123–125; addressing audience's
understanding, 129–131; academic, religious and political,
140
Rickert, Heinrich, 153
Ricoeur, Paul, xxviii
Rights, 87, 88, 97
Rilke, Rainer Maria, 141
Rilla, Walter and Paul, 141
Ritual, xxv
Romantics, x, 25, 89, 96
Rousseau, Jean-Jacques, 1, 24, 28,
60, 102, 111
Rules, 59, 121, 135

Saint-Simon, Comte de, 94
Schelling, Friedrich Wilhelm
Joseph von, 139
Schiller, Johann Christoph Fried-
rich von, 87, 92–93, 106, 121
Schleiermacher, Friedrich, 54
Schlick, Moritz, 53

About *Yale Studies in Hermeneutics*

Yale Studies in Hermeneutics provides a venue for inquiry into the theory of interpretation in all its varieties and domains. Titles in the series seek to expand and deepen our understanding of understanding while explicitly framing and situating themselves within the tradition of recognized hermeneutical thinkers from antiquity to the present.